78754

PR
6045
072Z815

Marder

Feminism & art

Date Due

MY 3 72	MAY 5 '80	MAY 23 '97	
FE 22 73	MAY 19 '80	JUL 8 9 97	
MY 22 73	JUN 0 '80	FEB 12 '98	
	MAY 13 '8	MAY 11	NOV 17
JE 12 7	JUN 14 '83	MAY 2	
NOV 3 75	JAN 2	APR 0 3 2001	
DEC 15 '75	MAR 2 7 199	APR 2 3 201	
OCT 27 76	4-1-92		
JAN 28 '78	OCT 4 1993		
MAY 17 7	JUN 0 6 1994		
APR 22 '80	NO 3 0 '95		

FEMINISM & ART

Herbert Marder

FEMINISM & ART

A Study of Virginia Woolf

The University of Chicago Press

Chicago and London

Library of Congress Catalog Card Number: 68-16704

The University of Chicago Press, Chicago 60637
The University of Chicago Press, Ltd., London W.C.1

If I am not for myself who is for me?

And when I am for myself what am I?

And if not now, when?

Hillel

Acknowledgments

I am grateful for help received from a number of individuals and institutions. Professors William York Tindall and John Unterecker gave me advice and encouragement when they were most needed. I am indebted to Dorothy Brewster, James Hafley, Carolyn Heilbrun, Kenneth Koch, Robert Maguire and Theodore Ziolkowski for constructive criticisms. The English Department of the University of Illinois generously made funds available for the preparation of the manuscript, and Stephen Zelnick helped with the index and other editorial matters.

Of the several valuable books about Virginia Woolf, James Hafley's excellent study, *The Glass Roof: Virginia Woolf as Novelist*, has taught me the most.

Passages from Aileen Pippett's *The Moth and the Star: A Biography of Virginia Woolf* are quoted by permission of Little, Brown and Company. Several paragraphs in Chapter Five have been adapted from an article, "Virginia Woolf's

Contents

Introduction

Virginia Woolf's feminism does not quite fit into the picture that most readers have of her. She is known, primarily, as an experimental novelist who perfected a form of interior monologue. Her name is frequently associated with some sort of esoteric cult: aestheticism, the Bloomsbury group. It is easy to see why many people assume, almost as a matter of course, that her novels must be devoid of social significance. The critics have done very little to challenge this assumption, in spite of E. M. Forster's reminder that "there are spots of [feminism] all over her work and it was constantly in her mind."[1] Most critics have emphasized the formal characteristics of her novels and passed over their connections with other writings, such as the feminist tracts. They have said little or nothing about the Virginia Woolf who prided herself on being called "the most brilliant pamphleteer in England."[2]

---

[1] *Virginia Woolf: The Rede Lecture* (Cambridge, 1942), pp. 22–23.
[2] *A Writer's Diary*, June 3, 1938, p. 234. For editions of Virginia Woolf's books quoted in this study, see the Bibliography.

I

This tendency to isolate the fiction from the work as a whole has to some degree prevented a full understanding of Virginia Woolf as an artist. She was certainly committed to an aesthetic that stressed the purity of the work of art. She was also deeply interested in social problems. She combined these characteristics in her own highly individual way. Virginia Woolf never succumbed to the temptation to turn the novel into a vehicle for propaganda, as did, for instance, D. H. Lawrence. On the other hand, her novels are very far from being "pure" works of art; there is, implicitly, a great deal of social criticism in them—a kind of latent propaganda. Virginia Woolf was perfectly capable of being doctrinaire, as her feminist essays show. Her desire to play the moralist was in conflict with her artistic conscience, and the conflict can be detected in almost everything she wrote.

The purpose of this book is to study the relation between Virginia Woolf's feminism and her art. I have attempted, in the process, to suggest the unity behind the diversity of her work as novelist, critic and pamphleteer. I have also found myself, to some extent, sketching a portrait of the artist as social critic. The word "feminism," accordingly, must be understood in its broadest sense—as referring to Mrs. Woolf's intense awareness of her identity as a woman, her interest in feminine problems. Its meaning should not be restricted to the advocacy of women's rights. The following chapters show that, far from being a mere excrescence on her work, feminism (in this larger sense) is essential to her conception of reality.

A Room of One's Own and *Three Guineas*, the long feminist essays in which she explained her doctrine, can be compared to Yeats's *A Vision*. They are serious parodies, statements of a highly personal vision parading as impersonal treatises. Like Yeats's system, which brought him "metaphors for poetry," Virginia Woolf's feminism contributed something essential to her artistic development. It enriched her fiction with a social and psychological metaphor. And it provided a necessary link with the world of the social scientist and the reformer.

According to her doctrine, the subjugation of women is a

central fact of history, a key to most of our social and psychological disorders. Western civilization has emphasized the (masculine) rational faculties to the exclusion of the (feminine) faculties of intuition. The Victorians—among them Virginia Woolf's father, Leslie Stephen—carried this one-sidedness to an extreme. Rejecting the feminine part of the psyche, they proved themselves to be barbarians in spite of their accomplishments.

Virginia Woolf found evidences of barbarism in every aspect of modern life. It took many forms: paternal tyranny in the home, male supremacy in the state, intellectual rigidity within the mind. Excessive "virility" was responsible, she maintained, for the rise of dictatorships and the horrors of war. In private life one-sidedness had caused modern man to feel that he was a stranger to those around him and to himself as well.

The way to remedy these evils, according to Virginia Woolf, is to let feminine influences act freely, both within society and within the individual. Our only hope, as far as she is concerned, lies in cooperation between the sexes, and the extent to which such cooperation actually exists is an index of the extent to which a society has become civilized. When the wife is permitted to administer the law of sympathy in the home, domestic harmony becomes possible. When women take part in national affairs the evils of politics are mitigated. When the individual learns to cultivate both masculine and feminine sides of his mind he approaches unity of being. Wholeness—integration of the personality—is the ultimate goal, and the symbol Virginia Woolf uses to represent this ideal condition is the androgynous mind, the mind in which masculine and feminine elements attain a perfect balance.

Her preoccupation with this ideal did not cause her to lose sight of practical realities. She held that social reform is a necessary first step on the way to creating new values. For how can women advance spiritually unless they are free? And once women are free, men too will learn to overcome their one-sidedness. As one feminist put it, women have to "bring the feminine principle into an entirely masculinized world

and thereby make the world human instead of only masculine."[3]

Bernard Blackstone has summarized the assumptions that
lie behind Virginia Woolf's particular kind of feminism.
Pointing out that there are two kinds of truth for her, the
masculine truth of reason and the feminine truth of the
imagination, he goes on to say that

together, these truths make up what she calls reality. There are
human beings who combine the male and female modes of
perception more impartially than others; these are the artists,
the poets and painters who mediate reality to us. They show us
how neither the rational nor the intuitive can get on without
the other. . . .

Virginia Woolf has been called a feminist. . . . But more truly
we might call her an androgynist, because she puts the emphasis
every time on what a man and woman have to give each other,
on the mystery of completion, and not on the discussion of
separate superiorities.[4]

Virginia Woolf's feminism, as this summary implies, grew
out of a desire for wholeness and harmony. She began by
emphasizing the injustices done to women, but she could not
stop there. She was too much of an "androgynist," too
troubled by the malaise of her time. Her protests were
related, in the first place, to personal grievances, the condition
of middle-class women like herself, but they ultimately took
on more universal significance. In *Three Guineas* she condemned the main tendencies of western civilization. In *The
Years* she confirmed her indictment and presented a vision of
a better world.

My discussion roughly follows her expanding frame of
reference. It begins by considering Virginia Woolf's ideas in
relation to social history and the feminist movement. Then,
seeking to mediate between social and literary criticism, it
branches out to examine her thinking on such questions as the
nature of the feminine mind and the "mystery of completion."

[3]   Alison Neilans, "Changes in Sex Morality," in *Our Freedom and
       Its Results*, ed. Ray Strachey (London, 1936), p. 186. The publisher
       was Leonard and Virginia Woolf's Hogarth Press.
[4]   *Virginia Woolf* (London, 1952), pp. 26, 31.

··◦⟨ I ⟩◦··

Causes

In the years immediately preceding Virginia Woolf's birth, the legal status of English women was essentially the same as it had been in the middle ages. Their rights as individuals were severely limited. Married women could not dispose of the money they earned, or enter into valid contracts. They could be deprived of a say in the upbringing of their children. In one celebrated case, a husband, upon being estranged from his wife, sent the children to live with his mistress and refused to permit the mother to see them. He was entirely within his rights, and the act which was passed in 1839 as a result of this case only permitted the Lord Chancellor to grant custody to the mother until the children were seven years old. The law continued to assume that there could be no divergence of interest between man and wife. A woman could not sue her husband or hold him to an agreement that would have been legally binding under any other circumstances. "By marriage," says Blackstone, "the very being or legal existence of the woman is suspended, or at least it is incorporated or consolidated into that of the husband, under whose wing, protection and cover she performs everything. . . . My wife and I are one and I am he."[1]

If these facts do not prove Virginia Woolf's claim that English women have always been an oppressed class, they at least suggest that the state was willing to aid and abet domestic tyranny. A distinction must be made, of course, between kinds of behavior that are legally permissible and kinds of behavior that are common or habitual. But where the law discriminates, people will usually be found to take advantage of the fact. Mid-nineteenth-century criminal records in England show an average of nearly fifteen hundred cases a year of aggravated assault committed by husbands against their wives. There must have been a great many more incidents that were never reported. No matter how brutally a husband treated his wife, she was legally bound to keep his house and share his bed.

Nevertheless, it is difficult to generalize about the position of women during this period. It was a time of social change. Whatever the restrictions placed upon Victorian women, there were also new opportunities open to them. Setting aside Victoria herself, the careers of the Brontë sisters, Florence Nightingale, Elizabeth Barrett Browning, and George Eliot show that a woman of genius was no longer doomed to die in obscurity and be buried at the crossroads, as Virginia Woolf said would have happened to Shakespeare's sister if she had had a gift for dramatic literature. There is another indication that Victorian women had some power and influence in the many reforms that were enacted during the last two decades of the nineteenth century, while Virginia Woolf was growing up. The year of her birth, 1882, was also the year of The Married Women's Property Act, an important step in the economic emancipation of women. One of its provisions was that "a married woman shall be capable of acquiring, holding and disposing by will . . . of any real or personal property as her separate property . . . without the intervention of any trustee."[2] Three years later,

[1]   Quoted by Ray Strachey, *The Cause* (London, 1928), p. 15.
[2]   Great Britain, *Parliamentary Papers* (1882), *Bills: Public*, vol. 4, p. 13.

a crusading newspaper editor revealed the existence of a thriving white slave trade which sent young British girls to houses of prostitution abroad. By setting the age of consent at thirteen, the law in effect encouraged seduction, making things easier for the pimps and madames. When this became widely known, the age of consent was raised to sixteen. The following year women for the first time won the right to act as guardians of their own children in case of the father's death. In 1891 the courts decided that "a husband had no right to carry off his wife by force or to imprison her until she submitted to his wishes."[3] If the British patriarch could no longer legally treat his wife as chattel, custom still gave him a powerful influence over all her actions. But by the beginning of this century, when Virginia Woolf was eighteen, "British women were, in the main, free, both in their persons and their properties . . . and the Women's Movement was nearing its height."[4]

The effects of this growing women's movement are apparent in the literature of the time. Many important writers were influenced by feminist ideas, and a significant part of the social criticism in Victorian novels has to do with the grievances of women. Novelists and poets created a succession of remarkable female characters such as Charlotte Brontë's Jane Eyre, Elizabeth Barrett Browning's Aurora Leigh, George Eliot's Dorothea Brooke, Thomas Hardy's Tess of the d'Urbervilles. Probably the most effective literary statement of the feminine dilemma was *A Doll's House*, which was first performed in 1879. The example of Ibsen's Nora could not be so easily ignored as the protests of feminists, and that is why *A Doll's House* aroused so much indignation among conservatives. More and more people were seeing the point, that although women might be quiet, they were not necessarily satisfied with their lot in life. Ibsen's conclusions were similar to those which Virginia Woolf stated, fifty years later, in *A Room of One's Own*. Jotting down some "Notes for the Modern Tragedy," before

3   W. Lyon Blease, *The Emancipation of English Women* (London, 1913), p. 140.
4   Strachey, *The Cause*, pp. 223-24.

beginning to write *A Doll's House*, Ibsen observed that there are two kinds of spiritual law, two kinds of conscience, one in man, and another, altogether different, in woman. They do not understand each other; but in practical life the woman is judged by man's law as though she were not a woman but a man.

The wife in the play ends by having no idea of what is right or wrong; natural feeling on the one hand, belief in authority on the other, have altogether bewildered her.

A woman cannot be herself in the society of the present day, which is exclusively masculine society, with laws framed by men and with a judicial system that judges feminine conduct from a masculine point of view.[5]

By the 1890's Ibsen's plays were being produced in London, where Hardy was shocking middle-class readers with his attacks on the prevailing sexual morality, and a self-styled Ibsenite, George Bernard Shaw, was writing *Mrs. Warren's Profession* and *Candida*.

The "new woman" was making her appearance in popular novels such as Grant Allen's *The Woman Who Did* and H. G. Wells's *Ann Veronica*. The provocative title of Allen's 1895 bestseller is a fair clue to its content. This book capitalized on advanced ideas about marriage and female emancipation by combining them with a melodramatic plot. H. G. Wells's heroine, like Grant Allen's, is determined to retain her independence and freedom of action, but both young women soon find themselves involved in love affairs, and events unfold in predictable fashion. There is an element in *Ann Veronica* which was absent from the earlier novel. While Herminia Barton of *The Woman Who Did* found it necessary to suffer alone for the sake of her principles, Ann Veronica, a few years later, can join a feminist society. When her love life becomes too complicated, she takes part in a militant protest which results in her being sent to prison. This is no tragedy, however, merely a prelude to connubial bliss.

Virginia Woolf (then Virginia Stephen) read Wells's books, and agreed with the liberal and high-minded senti-

---

5   Quoted by Donald Clive Stuart in *The Development of Dramatic Art* (New York, 1937), p. 575.

ments which they expressed. Nevertheless, she had reservations about Wells as a novelist because of what seemed to her his misguided attempts to combine art and propaganda.[6] Although she was determined to have her say in the controversy about women's rights, she was equally determined to keep didacticism out of her novels.

The generation to which Virginia Stephen belonged was the first to enjoy on a large scale the freedoms for which the feminists had been fighting. Her youth coincided with a turning point in the history of the feminist movement. She had been born early enough to know Victorian England from personal experience, as well as from contact with her elders. Her memories of that patriarchal society, ruled by a queen who was implacably hostile to the feminist movement, were vivid and disturbing. In their home life the Stephens, like most middle-class Victorian families, composed a patriarchal society in miniature. The father, a somewhat distant and majestic figure, was the center around whom everything revolved, the arbiter whose austere judgments shaped his ambitious daughter's opinion of herself. By the time that young girl had become a young woman her world had changed almost beyond recognition. Women had won the vote and penetrated the masculine professions. The girl herself was becoming known as a writer—a writer, moreover, whose aestheticism was at the furthest possible remove from her father's philosophy.

But such breaks with the past are rarely as complete as they seem. Leslie Stephen's daughter, like many of her contemporaries, rejected Victorian ideas of propriety, but in doing so she displayed a form of moral earnestness derived from the Victorians themselves. Her pursuit of the good and the beautiful was in keeping with her father's example; her intense intellectuality revealed the influence of that irascible and kindly old man. Her career itself seems vaguely to echo his. Leslie Stephen was an eminent man of letters who had

[6] See her well-known attacks on Wells, Galsworthy, Bennett, in "Modern Fiction," *The Common Reader*, and "Mr. Bennett and Mrs. Brown," *The Captain's Death Bed*.

overcome a nervous weakness in his youth by means of strict self-discipline. When Virginia was born, he was the editor of one of the most respected British periodicals, the *Cornhill Magazine*, and she grew up in the midst of fashionable literary society. The family's friends were dignitaries and famous men, such as James Russell Lowell (her godfather), Thomas Hardy, Henry James, George Meredith. In making her way in the world as a young woman, Virginia had to contend with her own mental instability. She managed, nevertheless, to establish herself at the center of literary society. Bloomsbury friends such as E. M. Forster, Lytton Strachey, Maynard Keynes, and Roger Fry formed a brilliant group, comparable to that which had frequented her father's house. The more closely one looks, the more clearly one perceives in her career, the effects of the training which she received as a girl. All of her attitudes, including her feminism, as it developed in later life, are related to this class and family background—particularly the influence of her father and his ideas.

One writer, in emphasizing the importance of this paternal inheritance, has pointed out that although "in her physical beauty, temperament and imagination she certainly resembled her mother . . . such an endowment may be greatly modified by environment. Leslie Stephen, like other strong, opinionated Victorian men, was a formidable piece of environment."[7] It must be kept in mind that her mother died when Virginia was thirteen. From that time until Leslie Stephen's death in 1904, he was the dominant influence in her life. After the loss of her mother, Virginia, who had always been delicate, suffered a nervous breakdown, and it was decided that she should be educated at home. Her father was her intellectual guide, she read the books on his shelves, and those which he brought home for her from the London Library. Leslie Stephen was a distinguished literary critic and biographer, as well as the historian of English thought in the eighteenth century and the utilitarians. Young Virginia read

[7] Hilda Ridley, "Leslie Stephen's Daughter," *Dalhousie Review*, 33 (Spring, 1953): 65.

all of English literature, and her first impressions were
colored by memories of her father's terse judgments, and his
disconcerting way of chanting poetry to himself. The fictional portrait which she drew of him many years after his
death in *To the Lighthouse* reveals the complexity of the
emotions which he aroused in her. She commented on his
influence—and her own ambivalence—in her dairy: "Father's
birthday. He would have been 96, 96, yes, today and could
have been 96, like other people one has known: but merci-
fully was not. His life would have entirely ended mine. What
would have happened? No writing, no books;—inconceiv-
able. . . . I must read him some day. I wonder if I can feel
again, I hear his voice, I know this by heart."[8] Especially in
his later years, Stephen was at times a household tyrant like
Mr. Ramsay. Within the limits determined by his principles,
he was a broadminded man, but his attitude toward women
and the family, like his relationship with his children, displays
some interesting contradictions.

As a political liberal Stephen believed that women should
be assured equality under the law. In writing the life of his
friend, Henry Fawcett, he described a point of view with
which he sympathized. Fawcett, he said, was "a chivalrous
supporter of women's rights." Whether or not women were
actually the equals of men in any particular field of endeavor
seemed to him beside the point. The competition should give
"the prize to the most vigorous, but [Fawcett] was righteously
indignant when it was so contrived as to impose additional
burdens on the feeblest." Stephen further explained his
friend's views in another passage: "He did not, I think,
anticipate any great change in the ordinary career of women
—he admitted that, for the most part, it would continue to
lie chiefly in the domestic circle; but his sense of justice re-
volted against the virtual condemnation of a large number
of women in every class to inability to use their faculties
freely."[9]

The cautiously progressive sentiments of this passage were

[8]   *A Writer's Diary*, November 28, 1928, p. 135.
[9]   *The Life of Henry Fawcett* (London, 1886), pp. 173, 177.

echoed by Stephen in his essay on "Forgotten Benefactors."
He was very willing to grant women all sorts of rights, but
he was not enthusiastic about the prospect of their using
them. He believed that women's place was in the home. This
attitude is implicit in an anecdote he told about a friend who
had confided to him that she felt ashamed when she compared the scope of her own work in the domestic sphere with
that of her husband, a politician. Stephen was not inclined to
see the matter in this light. He wrote:

No one, I hope, could assert more willingly than I, that the
faculties of women should be cultivated as fully as possible, and
that every sphere in which their faculties can be effectively
applied should be thrown open to them. But the doctrine
sometimes tacitly confounded with this, that the sphere
generally assigned to women is necessarily lower or less
important than others is not to be admitted. . . . The domestic
influence is, no doubt, confined within narrower limits; but
then, within those limits it is incomparably stronger and more
certain of effect. The man or woman can really mould the
character of a little circle, and determine the whole life of one
little section of the next generation.[10]

Stephen was more interested in defining the value of domestic
service than in considering the implications of his friend's
complaint. In proving the dignity and importance of
woman's work, he tended to ignore or minimize the dissatisfaction of the women who had to do it.

A belief in the importance of domestic life and the integrity
of the family formed an important part of Stephen's philosophy. In "Forgotten Benefactors" he wrote: "The degree in
which any ethical theory recognizes and reveals the essential
importance of the family relation is, I think, the best test of
its approximation to the truth. . . . To those activities which
knit families together, which help to enlarge the highest ideal
of domestic life, we owe a greater debt than to any other
kind of conduct. . . . The highest services of this kind are
rendered by persons condemned, or perhaps I should say
privileged, to live in obscurity."[11] Whatever his sympathy

10   *Social Rights and Duties* (London, 1896), 2: 249-51.
11   *Ibid.*, 2: 244, 245-46.

for women who felt that they had been prevented from using or developing their faculties, Stephen could not whole-heartedly support reforms that would give them a chance to do so. The family relation was of paramount importance to him, and domestic life, as he understood it, could not exist unless women stayed at home.

In another passage of "Forgotten Benefactors," Stephen expressed his veneration for his second wife, the mother of Virginia and the prototype of Mrs. Ramsay. "A lofty nature which has profited by passing through the furnace acquires claims not only upon our love but upon our reverence. . . . We cannot attempt to calculate the value of this spiritual force which has moulded our lives, which has helped by a simple consciousness of its existence to make us gentler, nobler, and purer in our thoughts of the world . . . which has constantly set before us a loftier ideal than we could frame for ourselves."[12] He went on to liken this ennobling influence to the light of the sun, of whose essential importance to us "we are apt to be unconscious . . . until some accident makes us realize the effect of its eclipse." In a letter written to his children after the death of his second wife he ranked her achievement in life high above his own: "Had I fully suc-ceeded and surpassed all my contemporaries in my own line, what should I have done? I should have written a book or two which might be read by my contemporaries and perhaps by the next generation. . . . Now I say, advisedly, that I do not think such an achievement as valuable as hers."[13] "That man is unfortunate," he believed, "who has not a saint of his own."[14]

Leslie Stephen's veneration of his second wife, and the im-portance which he attributed to the domestic sphere were obviously related. The home was the precinct in which his saint was enshrined; its existence made possible the operation of her special kind of sanctity. The family was needed to call forth her qualities, as she was needed to fill it with her

---

[12]   *Ibid.*, 2: 256, 258.
[13]   Quoted by Desmond MacCarthy in *Memories* (New York, 1953), pp. 93–94.
[14]   "Forgotten Benefactors," *Social Rights and Duties*, 2: 264.

ennobling influence. But a desire to worship woman as a higher moral influence tends, in real life, to restrict her freedom almost as much as a conviction of her inferiority. It is not uncommon to wish one's saint to remain on her pedestal so that one can go on worshipping her. The Victorian father often claimed to be protecting his wife or daughter when he was really protecting his image of her. Leslie Stephen, though on the whole a reasonable man, was capable of becoming a grim and threatening incarnation of the Victorian father.

As far as sex was concerned Stephen's position was that of the strict moralist. Once again, his strictures were connected with his belief in the importance of the domestic sphere, for sexual purity was the basis of stable family life. Noël Annan says as much in his study of Stephen: "Like other Victorian moralists [Stephen] sees loose-living and lust as the hooks which clutch at man and make him lower than the angels. Man can be saved from himself by woman: feminine innocence will rouse man from sensuality. . . . Because the institutions of marriage and the family will perish, and society with them, unless we eradicate 'brutalizing and anti-social instincts' all social forces must be directed to the inculcation of chastity."[15] The pattern is clear: the need to believe in the moral superiority of women; the faith in the sanctity of the family; the prohibition against loose-living lest the purity of women and the stability of the home be endangered—these attitudes made Leslie Stephen cling to the Victorian proprieties. He remained faithful, emotionally at least, to the old order which was rapidly becoming a thing of the past.

Stephen's attitude toward sex also entered into his position as a critic. He prized masculinity very highly and despised effeminacy. Thus, one of the most serious defects which he found in the works of such women novelists as the Brontës and George Eliot was their failure to create believable male characters. Their "men were often simply women in disguise."[16] The corresponding failures of male writers to create

[15] *Leslie Stephen: His Thought and Character in Relation to His Time* (Cambridge, Mass., 1952), p. 228.

[16] "George Eliot," *Hours in a Library* (New York, 1904), 4: 163.

plausible female characters seem to have troubled him far less. For Leslie Stephen, writes Annan, "the opposite of masculine is not feminine but morbid."[17]

Stephen's response to effeminacy was that of the red-blooded Victorian Englishman. The slightest hint of inversion provoked the bully in him. In her mature years Virginia Woolf rebelled against this attitude. Her circle of artists and intellectuals included a number of homosexuals, and she and her friends took it for granted that a person's sex life is a private matter concerning only himself. Leslie Stephen's whole concept of sexual attributes, and especially his belief in the importance of masculinity, was repugnant to her. But while she rejected her father's ideas, Virginia Woolf found it harder to discard the emotional legacy he had left her. Here and there in her books she displays traces of severity, not to say priggishness, befitting the daughter of a knighted Victorian moralist. Her novels, too, are marked by a more than average reticence about sex. Leslie Stephen measured the value of works of art by their moral significance. His daughter's aestheticism, like her belief in sexual freedom, contained a considerable degree of ambivalence. Perhaps it is precisely because her aestheticism was an overreaction against her father's moralizing that she could not, within its limits, do full justice either to her social interests or her artistic values. The need to moralize remained strong in her, but it was submerged and displaced. In the 1920's, and even later, when she had become a novelist with an international reputation, she still carried on the struggle with her father's ghost. The composition of *To the Lighthouse*, with its fictionalized portraits of both her parents, was a rite she needed to perform in order to free herself. "I used to think of him and mother daily," she noted, ". . . I was obsessed by them both, unhealthily; and writing of them was a necessary act."[18] Shortly after finishing *To the Lighthouse* she produced her most extravagant book, *Orlando*, and wrote in *A Room of One's Own* that the creative faculty is based on the union of masculine and feminine

17   *Leslie Stephen*, p. 226.
18   *A Writer's Diary*, November 28, 1928, p. 135.

elements. The artist's mind is androgynous, and not, as Leslie Stephen had contended, solidly masculine or feminine.

In 1932 Virginia Woolf wrote a brief reminiscence of her father. She described him affectionately but with a considerable degree of detachment. He was a man, she said, who could be alarmingly opinionated and admirably magnanimous, who inspired both love and resentment. "His daughters, though he cared little enough for the higher education of women," had the same freedom as his sons to follow whatever professions they chose. "If at one moment he rebuked a daughter sharply for smoking a cigarette—smoking was not in his opinion a nice habit in the other sex—she had only to ask him if she might become a painter, and he assured her that so long as she took her work seriously he would give her all the help he could. He had no special love for painting; but he kept his word. Freedom of that sort was worth thousands of cigarettes."[19] After the death of her father, Virginia Woolf became a habitual smoker of cigars.

The generation to which Virginia Woolf belonged was in revolt against Victorianism. Mrs. Woolf was extremely sensitive to the present, that is to say, to the spirit of modernism. She was also linked to the past by unusually strong bonds. Her father had believed in a certain kind of moral strenuousness, and although Virginia and her friends were serious young people, it was almost a point of honor with them to

[19]   "Leslie Stephen" in *The Captain's Death Bed*, p. 71. In spite of Leslie Stephen's tolerance of his daughter's artistic ambitions, he appears at times to have been less than reasonable. "When Stephen discusses sex," Noël Annan observes, "he begins to shriek: then he rushes in, fists milling, like a small boy in a temper, and most of his blows go wide" (*Leslie Stephen*, p. 229). Aileen Pippett recounts a typical incident in the family life of the Stephens, after Virginia's mother had died: "When her father made a scene and almost reduced Vanessa to tears, it was terrible for Virginia to have to excuse him for being so majestic and so unreasonable. It was also belittling to his real dignity that they knew he would be sorry later on and would reproach himself bitterly and need to be comforted because he was such an unkind father." *The Moth and the Star: A Biography of Virginia Woolf* (Boston, 1955), p. 26.

adopt an attitude as far removed as possible from that of their elders. Here is the way John Maynard Keynes expressed it in an essay entitled, "My Early Beliefs": "We repudiated entirely customary morals, conventions, and traditional wisdom. We were, that is to say, in the strict sense of the term, immoralists. We recognized no moral obligation on us, no inner sanction, to conform or to obey."[20] Virginia Woolf's iconoclasm differed somewhat from that of her friends in being based on a feminist rationale. Moreover, her commitment to the present was modified by her need to preserve her ties with the past. This conjunction of modernism and traditionalism was responsible for the characteristic tone of her prose, and for its special fascination.

Almost every writer on Virginia Woolf has commented on the fundamental dualism in her work. Unlike some of her contemporaries, she wished not only to criticize the tradition which she had inherited, but in a sense to renew it. Her goal was to write in such a way as to satisfy the utilitarian philosophy of her father, while remaining true to the artistic mood of her own generation. The former demanded that her books contribute something to the welfare of mankind, the latter taught her that every work of art is autonomous, a purely aesthetic skirmish in the struggle to achieve "significant form." The moralist in Virginia Woolf is most in evidence in her feminist writings, and the aesthete in her novels; neither is entirely lacking in anything she wrote.[21]

---

[20]   *Essays and Sketches in Biography* (New York, 1956), p. 252.
[21]   Clive Bell comments on Virginia Woolf's occasional tendency to discourage her friends from pursuing the arts: "Sometimes it seemed to me that Virginia had inherited from her immediate ancestors more than their beauty and intelligence. Every good Victorian knew that a young man should have a sensible profession, something solid and secure, which would lead naturally to a comfortable old age and a fair provision for the children. In her head Virginia knew perfectly well that to give such advice to Lytton [Strachey] or Duncan [Grant] was absurd; but Virginia, like the merest man, was not always guided by reason." *Old Friends* (New York, 1957), p. 100.

2

Leslie Stephen's death in 1904 led to a dramatic change in his daughter's way of life. She moved from Kensington to Bloomsbury, that is, from middle-class domestication to high-brow bohemianism. Other things being equal, there is no doubt about which of these worlds she preferred. The loss of her father was a harrowing experience, but in later life she looked back upon it almost with a sense of relief. As she observed in her diary,[22] she was now free to have the career that would otherwise have been denied her. The four orphaned Stephen children, all in their twenties, set up house together. Soon Virginia was getting to know a group of Thoby's brilliant Cambridge friends, among them Leonard Woolf, her future husband. The sensitive, sheltered girl suddenly found herself an independent woman who could earn one pound ten shillings and sixpence by scribbling a few pages and sending them to an editor, a fact that amazed and delighted her. She sold her first reviews and was encouraged to think seriously of becoming a writer.

This crucial moment in Virginia Stephen's life coincided, almost exactly, with the beginning of the heroic phase of the women's movement. Suffrage societies had been in existence for about forty years, but they had attracted relatively little attention. In 1903 a new society, the Women's Social and Political Union (WSPU) was founded by Emmeline Pankhurst in Manchester. Mrs. Pankhurst and her followers were radicals. They believed that women must fight for their emancipation, using whatever means were available to them. To be sure, they could not overthrow the government, but they could infiltrate meetings and heckle speakers who were opposed to their cause. They could demand that every candidate for public office commit himself on the subject of women's rights. They could march on Parliament in tens of thousands, provoking the police to arrest them and filling the prisons. In short, they could keep up a steady, vigorous harassment of the authorities who had prevented women's suffrage bills from being enacted in Parliament. Mrs. Pank-

[22] See p. 11 above.

hurst's militant policy came to be self-sustaining. The more violent the militants grew, the more police action they provoked, the more publicity they attracted. Notoriety did no harm at all to the WSPU; its membership grew rapidly. Money flowed into the national office, making possible still more spectacular protests which in their turn generated still more publicity. With its emphasis on civil disobedience, Mrs. Pankhurst's movement inevitably produced its martyrs: one woman threw herself under the horses' hoofs at a fashionable race course and was killed. Many others, imprisoned for resisting police or throwing rocks through windows, went on hunger strikes and were forcibly fed. For nine years, from 1905 to 1914, the militants kept the cause of women's rights in the public eye. Again and again their demands were rejected, but it was impossible to ignore them, or to deny the fanatical heroism of their leaders.

The period 1911-13, when the militant agitation reached its peak, was another time of transition for Virginia Stephen. In 1912, the year of her marriage to Leonard Woolf, social critic and socialist, she was thirty years old and finishing her first novel.[23] As her husband soon discovered, Virginia Woolf's mental equilibrium, which had broken down several times during her youth, was still extremely precarious. Not only did the condition of her health preclude any strenuous activity, such as taking part in protests and rallies, but it made even a normal active life potentially dangerous. She would always have to avoid undue excitement.

Leonard Woolf has movingly described his wife's mental illness and the precautions which they had to take throughout their married life. As long as Virginia Woolf lived "a quiet, vegetative life, eating well, going to bed early . . . she remained perfectly well."[24] But if she were subjected to any mental or physical strain "serious danger signals" would

---

[23] *The Voyage Out* was completed in February, 1913, and published in 1915. See Leonard Woolf, *Beginning Again* (New York, 1964), p. 87.

[24] *Ibid.*, p. 76.

appear—"a peculiar 'headache' low down at the back of the head, insomnia, and a tendency for the thoughts to race." If these symptoms were not checked at once by rest and seclusion in a darkened room they would grow much worse. Four times in her life they led to nervous breakdowns which continued for months or years. An attack came on not long after her marriage. At one point she fell into a coma for two days and at another tried to commit suicide by taking an overdose of veronal. While in the depressive state, she was subject to delusions and fits of violence, and required the care of two trained nurses. There was constant danger, during these periods of insanity, that she would try to kill herself.

Aside from her health, there was another important factor which kept Virginia Woolf from joining public demonstrations. As much as she sympathized with the aims of the suffragists, she could not share their enthusiasm for political action; she found something antipathetic in the idea of marching in a protest or even sitting on a committee. She was a lady and a highbrow—aristocratic, aloof. On the other hand, she was unusually sensitive to any slight on account of her sex. The mere thought of being discriminated against could make her physically ill. This extreme sensitivity brought her close, at times, to the militant suffragists, though she differed from them in many of her assumptions.

Her attitude toward the question of women's rights was never simple and straightforward. Her energies were directed differently from the majority of feminists who were concerned mainly with eliminating specific abuses and not much interested in trying to discover the causes of tyranny. If her attitude was less practical than theirs, her vision was more comprehensive. Long after women had won the vote she was at work with her pen, shaping a role for herself, making her own contribution to "The Cause." Her labors resulted in the two long and impassioned essays, *A Room of One's Own* and *Three Guineas*. These books are not merely tracts, but, in one way or another, touch on all the matters that vitally concerned her. And because she would never restrict herself to one genre at a time, they often have something in common with her novels. The tracts fade into fiction, the fiction echoes

the tracts; and the continuity is so pronounced that it seems necessary to read every book by Virginia Woolf in the context of her work as a whole. Her attitude as a feminist was intimately bound up with her attitude as an artist. When we unravel the intricacies and describe the contradictions of the one, we are led toward an understanding of the other.

Virginia Woolf's first two novels contain most of the important themes of her fiction, themes which reveal her preoccupation with the problems of women. They also seem to reveal uncertainties connected with her early married life. The heroines of *The Voyage Out* and *Night and Day* are both afraid to marry. In each case the crucial question is whether a young woman can succeed in satisfying her emotional and intellectual needs within the framework of married life. The question is never satisfactorily answered. The conclusion of *The Voyage Out* seems, from one point of view, to reflect an inability to come to grips with the heroine's dilemma. Rachel Vinrace, a talented girl devoted to her books and music—and given to dreaming—goes on a voyage to South America, where she meets, and eventually becomes engaged to, an aesthetic young man. The lovers are dismayed by the social pressures on them to transform their relationship into a conventional courtship. They are deeply apprehensive about marriage, but before they can discover whether their fears are justified, Rachel grows ill and dies. This ending, which emphasizes the arbitrariness of fate, is not altogether satisfactory. The reader suspects that Rachel was too jealous of her independence to marry anyone, and that the novelist has evaded the implications of this fact. One critic has summed up the theme as "the hestitation a girl of spirit and breeding felt at yielding in marriage to one of the traditionally dominant sex."[25]

Night and Day deals even more explicitly with the problems of marriage. In general outline it is a social comedy about lovers who are separated by a series of misunderstandings,

[25] Edwin Berry Burgum, "Virginia Woolf and the Empty Room," *The Novel and the World's Dilemma* (New York, 1947), p. 125.

and finally united when their true feelings become known. But *Night and Day* is more reminiscent of one of Shaw's problem plays than it is of *Evelina* or *Pride and Prejudice*. It is an intellectual romance. The main obstacle separating the lovers is Katharine Hilbery's inability to make up her mind, because what she wants out of life is apparently so different from what society expects her to want. Like Rachel Vinrace, she is terrified of marriage. She is so confused, moreover, that she has permitted herself to become engaged to a conventional male who expects his wife to devote herself to raising children and managing servants. Katharine finally escapes this life by breaking off her engagement and marrying Ralph Denham, an angry young man who believes that men and women need not interfere with each other even though married. *Night and Day* is a kind of fictional laboratory in which the author is testing ways of adapting old social forms to new needs. Unfortunately, Virginia Woolf once again stops short of answering the crucial question. Katharine and Ralph's experiment, the marriage in which they are to live both together and apart, is to take place in a nebulous future after the close of the novel. Like *The Voyage Out*, *Night and Day* ends with an evasion.

The feminist movement is a definite presence in both these books. In *Night and Day* one of the main characters works as the unpaid secretary of a suffrage society. Having been disappointed in love, Mary Datchet decides to devote her life to the cause, to become a professional feminist. Virginia Woolf contrasts the drab existence of the social reformer with Katharine's more glamorous private experiment in self-reform. Mary's suffrage society is mainly an object of satire. The total effect is interesting; women's problems are taken seriously, but the feminist societies are not. Both too much and too little is made of feminism as a theme—too much for it to remain mere background; too little for it to become a significant part of the fictional pattern. It seems that the writer has failed to resolve her own uncertainties and achieve a coherent point of view.

In method and outlook *The Voyage Out* and *Night and Day* belong to the pre-1914 era. But most of Virginia Woolf's

working life fell in the interim between the two world wars, in the years after women had won the vote. And after her first novels she rarely commented directly on social problems in her fiction. She confined such comments to the essays she regularly wrote. Works of art, she believed, should say what cannot be said by other means. They should reveal the hidden realities from which social problems spring, without engaging in social analysis. Virginia Woolf tried in her mature novels to penetrate unexplored regions of the ordinary and habitual. Fear and tyranny begin, she observed, in the casual moments that compose people's lives from hour to hour, from day to day. The most esoteric truths are concealed in the most commonplace experiences. As she pursued these truths, Virginia Woolf's novels became increasingly plotless, fragmented, and evocative.

Night and Day had dealt with the problem of marriage somewhat analytically—by isolating it for study. *Mrs. Dalloway* and *To the Lighthouse* dealt with it impressionistically. These novels of the decade following World War I contain vivid pictures of family life and domestic tyranny, but they do not converge on a central "problem." Virginia Woolf was attempting here to capture moments of sensibility in order to reveal the inner lives of her characters. She wished to convey, as precisely as possible, what it feels like to be a particular individual—Clarissa Dalloway or Mrs. Ramsay— at half past two on an ordinary day. Her awareness of social problems is still present, but it has been absorbed into a broader range of ideas, connected with many levels of experience. The advantage lies with the maturer novels. There is more reality in the delicate impressions and convolutions of *To the Lighthouse* than in the elaborate representation of *Night and Day*. Nevertheless, in spite of this new emphasis on the texture of experience, Virginia Woolf never allows us to forget that her characters have suffered certain disadvantages, if women, and enjoyed certain privileges, if men. The essential differences between these two "classes," as she called them, were always on her mind.

In *Mrs. Dalloway* and *To the Lighthouse* it is mainly her descriptions of masculine tyranny which remind us that

23

Virginia Woolf was a feminist. These books of her middle period reveal an increasing interest in the minds of the oppressors. The desire for power over others, she seems to be saying, always does incalculable harm. One suspects that Mr. Ramsay, for instance, is at least partially responsible for his wife's untimely death. An even more representative patriarch is Sir William Bradshaw, the fashionable doctor whose insensitivity plays a decisive part in causing the suicide of Septimus Smith. Behind these portraits there is a sense of general evil: Septimus has been shellshocked in a war that confirmed the feminist charge of masculine brutality. Virginia Woolf's preoccupation with the causes of this evil finally led her beyond the bounds of fiction.

Having completed *To the Lighthouse* she began working on a fantasy in a much lighter vein, which became *Orlando*. At the same time she was preparing two lectures, delivered at Newnham and Girton in 1928, which became the basis of *A Room of One's Own*. *Orlando* and *A Room of One's Own* represent a summing up of Virginia Woolf's feminist ideas as of the late twenties. The two books have in common not only their emphasis on the bi-sexuality of the artist but their good humor and whimsicality; in writing *A Room of One's Own* Virginia Woolf was fully aware of the dangers that beset the controversialist and made every effort to avoid them. But, though she carefully excluded strident tones, her commitment to the cause of women's rights was perfectly serious.

In *Orlando*, fantasy became a means of emphasizing the inner life of her hero-heroine; liberated from the demands of strict rationality, Virginia Woolf could glance satirically at the position of women in different ages and poke fun at masculine pedantry. Orlando's famous change of sex about halfway through the novel allowed her to comment shrewdly on relations between the sexes. It is only in *A Room of One's Own*, however, that the broader outlines of her feminist doctrine begin to appear. The original subject of the lectures here revised and expanded was "Women and Fiction," but Virginia Woolf had used this subject as a point of departure for a general discussion of the woman question. The resulting tract, constantly enlivened, or diluted, with fiction, can be described as a feminist fantasy. It begins with the story of a visit to two colleges, one for men, the other for women. In the men's college, the narrator says, she dined on sole, partridge, and "a confection which rose all sugar from the waves." The same evening, in the dining hall of the women's college, she had been served a supper of beef, custard and prunes. Two scenes had been evoked in her mind, the first of "kings and nobles" bringing "treasure in huge sacks" and the second of "lean cows and a muddy market and withered greens."

Virginia Woolf's main contention in this book is that in order to write "a woman must have money and a room of her own." That is, she must have the same opportunities as men to pursue her interests, to be free of material cares. Trying to answer the question, "Why are women so poor?" Virginia Woolf discusses the trouble they have had in earning a living. She comments indignantly on the position of English women at various times in history and glances at the books written about them, mainly by men. On the whole, women have failed to create great works of art, she says, because they have been denied an opportunity to develop their faculties. The one field in which they have made substantial contributions is literature—and for very good reasons. It was possible to keep them out of academies and institutes, but no one could bar them from the writing-desk or forbid the use of pen and paper. Nevertheless, in spite of the genius of women like Jane Austen, George Eliot, the Brontës, the exploration of truly feminine modes of expression has never seriously been attempted. Such an undertaking, Virginia Woolf predicted, would have important implications for the art of fiction as a whole. Here her feminism and her attitude as a critic came into conjunction. For she believed that novelists, especially women novelists, had often been misled by the prevailing masculine bias, and that in order for creation to take place there must be a meeting, a fusion of masculine and feminine elements. One-sidedness causes the spirit to atrophy. Ideally, the artist should be androgynous, like Orlando. Virginia Woolf concluded,

25

therefore, by emphasizing the importance of cooperation between the sexes. She looked forward to a time when life would become ordered and harmonious, when men and women would finally succeed in sharing their wisdom.

On the whole *A Room of One's Own* creates an impression of wit and urbanity. In spite of misgivings about the patriarchs, Virginia Woolf could still permit herself to be optimistic. In her later works this was no longer true. As the 1930's wore on she became increasingly appalled by social injustice. She could not look at the world with equanimity. Her old horror of masculine authority was magnified by constant reports of tyranny and aggression. She no longer felt the inclination to indulge in literary "escapades," such as the one that had produced *Orlando*. She could not be good-humored about concentration camps, and she was more concerned than ever about injustices to women. For the condition of her sex seemed to her a sign of a universal danger that was growing steadily greater.

The Years and *Three Guineas*, works which are the culmination of her writings on women, reveal this darker mood. Published in 1937 and 1938, they may be considered companion volumes, like *Orlando* and *A Room of One's Own*: Virginia Woolf actually referred to them as "one book" in her diary.[26] These two pairs of companion volumes complement each other, presenting her ideas about women from different points of view. They range from sociology to fictional biography, from saga to fantasy, and occasionally approach poetry. Between them they contain essentially all of Virginia Woolf's ideas about the position of women. *A Room of One's Own* and *Three Guineas* are deliberate formulations of these ideas; *Orlando* and *The Years* are fictional and

[26] "That's the end of six years floundering, striving, much agony, some ecstasy: lumping *The Years* and *Three Guineas* together as one book—as indeed they are." *A Writer's Diary*, June 3, 1938, p. 284. Cf. the entry for May 21, 1935 (pp. 240-41): "Oddities of the human brain: woke early and again considered dashing off my book on Professions [*Three Guineas*], to which I had not given a single thought these 7 or 8 days. Why? This vacillates with my novel [*The Years*]—how are they both to come out simultaneously."

do not teach anything (Virginia Woolf was a firm believer in the separation of art and propaganda) but nevertheless reflect the thought of the essays. While *Orlando* and *A Room of One's Own* pay a great deal of attention to the inner life, the emphasis in the two later books is explicitly on women in relation to society. Their total effect, however, is not to exclude psychological comment; on the contrary, in *The Years* Virginia Woolf succeeded brilliantly in revealing the minds of her characters by indirect methods.

The Years is a fictional saga tracing the disappearance of the Victorian system of family life which had been described in *To The Lighthouse*; it is documentation, in a sense, for *Three Guineas*, in which Virginia Woolf formulated a feminist program based on her observations of society. To put it another way, we can infer the state of mind that inspired the program set forth in *Three Guineas* from this grim view of society. The novel follows members of three related family groups from 1880 to "the present day," that is, 1937. The Victorian family (the Pargiters have seven children), which seems to be so stable at the beginning of the novel, is shown to be in a state of decadence. The father visits his mistress while his wife lies dying; the daughters are frustrated and desperate. Although the rituals of respectability continue to be practiced, no one is quite sure any longer what they mean. People hide their dissatisfaction, even from themselves; Victorian society is sinister—a world in which lies fester. By the end of the novel the various family groups have been all but disbanded, many of the children have remained unmarried, most are living in isolation; the evils inherent in the old tradition have done their work. In the last chapter all the surviving characters and their children and grandchildren gather at a party, a kind of family reunion, which serves to sharpen our sense of time passing and of that revolution in society which has shaken and dispersed the Pargiters.

Given the simple chronological scheme of *The Years* and its emphasis on physical realities, it was possible for Virginia Woolf to bring in the movement for social and political reforms in a way that would have been jarring in her earlier novels. Eleanor is active in philanthropic organizations and

27

the feminist movement; one sister has romantic dreams of becoming a revolutionary; another goes to jail as a suffragette. Changes in the status of women are suggested during the finale by the introduction of Eleanor's niece—a young lady doctor who is dedicated to her work and interested in little else. An awareness of political and social issues pervades *The Years*, as it does so many works of the thirties. The reforming societies, moreover, in spite of their activity, have not succeeded in getting at the root of the problem, and we are aware, as the book closes, that England is threatened by dictatorship from abroad.

The rise of fascism appalled Virginia Woolf. She consistently interpreted this political development in terms of her ideas about the position of women. Thus, when she set out to discuss the causes of the European crisis in *Three Guineas*, the book, as it were of itself, became an exposition of feminist doctrine. Improving the lot of women and opposing tyranny were identified in her mind. The early feminists had been fighting in essentially the same cause, she maintained, as contemporary democrats and anti-fascists.

Three Guineas opens with an anecdote. Virginia Woolf has received a letter asking her to contribute to a society for the prevention of war. The book is in the form of a reply, explaining why she has decided to send money elsewhere first—to a fund for rebuilding a women's college, to a society for helping women enter the professions—before considering the appeal of the antiwar society. Her position is that the causes of war are to be found in the conventional education given to young people. They are brought up, for instance, to accept the exploitation of the female sex. Furthermore, women are excluded from national office, which results in an imbalance in the state, an inherent bias in favor of masculine traits such as acquisitiveness and pugnacity. The evil must be attacked, she concludes, at the points where it originates. The "room of one's own" demanded in the earlier tract here has become an education that accords realistically with the feminine nature; the emphasis on an independent income has been transformed into an appeal for equal opportunity in the professions. In the course of her argument Virginia Woolf presents a documented survey of women's grievances. She casts a critical eye on essentially masculine institutions, such as the universities, the church, the army, and asserts that the fascist state is the apotheosis of virility. Finally she presents a series of practical proposals to the "daughters of educated men" based on her contention that woman has always been essentially an "outsider," a second-class citizen deprived of wealth and power. The exclusion of women from leadership in the state has helped them to preserve their moral superiority and fitted them to undertake a civilizing mission. Women in the professions, she says, should form a new, semi-monastic, noncompetitive order; they should help to educate young people in the arts of peace. Since they are by nature pacifists, they should engage in passive resistance to all preparations for war and refuse in any way to abet the belligerent males. If necessary, women should decline, like Lysistrata, to breed sons for cannon fodder.

Both *A Room of One's Own* and *Three Guineas* were written at a time when the ardor of the feminists had died down and public interest had waned. In 1936 one feminist leader wrote: "Modern young women know amazingly little of what life was like before the war, and show a strong hostility to the word 'feminism' and all which they imagine it to connote."[27] For many young women feminism was a dead issue, or perhaps a kind of reproach—something they had to live down. For Virginia Woolf, who belonged to an earlier generation, it was still very much alive. The world crisis, which made the claims of the feminists seem trivial to most people, only confirmed for her the importance of the women's movement. She was deeply interested in social and political issues, but she brought her own interpretation of history to bear on them. The position of her sex was a principle axis along which she attempted to plot contemporary events. Attitudes deriving from the pre-World War I era of militant feminism seem to have remained latent in her, coming to the surface during the twenties and thirties. She

[27]   Ray Strachey, "Introduction," *Our Freedom and Its Results* (London, 1936), p. 10.

had never had a chance to work off her resentments in political action. E. M. Forster may have been implying something of the kind when he said, a bit apologetically: "In my judgment there is something old-fashioned about this extreme feminism; it dates back to her suffragette youth of the 1910's, when men kissed girls to distract them from wanting the vote, and very properly provoked her wrath."[28] We must come back to the fact that Virginia Woolf's youth coincided with the pioneering era of feminism in order to see her attacks on the patriarchy in perspective. When she touched on the subject of women's rights, she frequently displayed the intensity, the touchiness, the "angularity," as she herself expressed it, of the pioneer.

Virginia Woolf considered the subjugation of women both cause and symptom of a fundamental imbalance in society. Her concern began with a sense of personal grievance; it ended with a consciousness of public responsibility. Inequality in the home had its counterpart in the political sphere; the problems of the family reflected those of the state. Lack of wholeness in the modern world was an implicit theme in almost everything she wrote. In her books she attempted to reconcile fact and imagination, masculine reason and feminine intuition. The following chapters are about her efforts to do so.

[28]   "Virginia Woolf," *Two Cheers for Democracy* (New York, 1951), p. 255.

·•⋑[2]⋐•·

The Decline of Family Happiness

Family life in England underwent great changes in Virginia Woolf's lifetime. She was born at the height of Victoria's reign and died during World War II. The outbreak of World War I, which marked the end of an era, divided her life almost in half. The prewar and postwar stages of her life correspond, roughly speaking, to two stages of family life described in her works. In the first stage the family still seems part of a stable social order, though signs of strain are beginning to appear. In the second stage, the traditional institutions are crumbling, and we see people living amidst "scraps, orts and fragments" of the old order. Virginia Woolf's pictures of family life contain an implicit evaluation of that order, and they place the confusion of the present in perspective against the way of life from which it grew. All her pictures of the family give us a sense of change rather than permanence.

Virginia Woolf was acutely conscious of the extent to which society had been transformed during her lifetime. In 1924 she wrote, "All human relations have shifted—those

between masters and servants, husbands and wives, parents
and children. And when human relations change there is at
the same time a change in religion, conduct, politics and
literature." Characteristically, she summed up the situation
in a phrase: "in or about December, 1910, human character
changed." To make her meaning clearer she gave an example: "The Victorian cook lived like a leviathan in the
lower depths, formidable, silent, obscure, inscrutable; the
Georgian cook is a creature of sunshine and fresh air; in and
out of the drawing-room, now to borrow the *Daily Herald*,
now to ask advice about a hat."[1] The form of her remarks is
playful, but she took the subject seriously.

Virginia Woolf was unable to take the family for granted,
as earlier novelists had done. She was impelled to reflect consciously about it as an institution. In most eighteenth- and
nineteenth-century novels, moral judgments had been made
against the background of more or less fixed social forms. In
Virginia Woolf's time the social background was changing
profoundly. Her novels not only described the behaviour of
individuals in society but included an implicit criticism of
social forms themselves.[2]

Virginia Woolf defined the fundamental nature of domestic life in *Night and Day*, contrasting it with the life of
thought, and especially with science. Katharine Hilbery, the
heroine, has been brought up to devote her life to pouring
tea and furthering the conversation of men. Katharine is

---

[1] "Mr. Bennett and Mrs. Brown," *The Captain's Death Bed*, pp. 91,
    92.
[2] In her essay on "Women and Fiction," Virginia Woolf predicted
    that in the future, women novelists would increasingly turn to
    social criticism. "The change which has turned the English woman
    from a nondescript influence, fluctuating and vague, to a voter, a
    wage-earner, a responsible citizen, has given her both in her life
    and in her art a turn toward the impersonal. Her relations now are
    not only emotional; they are intellectual, they are political. . . .
    Hence her attention is being directed away from the personal
    center which engaged it exclusively in the past to the impersonal,
    and her novels naturally became more critical of society, and less
    analytical of individual lives" (*Granite and Rainbow*, p. 83).

strongly individual, intelligent, and deeply uneasy; she is suffering from an overdose of domesticity. The antidote she chooses is the study of mathematics. She begins to fall in love with Ralph Denham when he speaks to her of his hobby, botany, and permits her to escape with him from the world of personal relations which confuses and terrifies her.

She wished he would go on forever talking of plants, and showing her how science felt not quite blindly for the law that ruled their endless variations. A law that might be inscrutable but was certainly omnipotent appealed to her at the moment, because she could find nothing like it in possession of human lives. Circumstances had long forced her, as they force most women in the flower of youth, to consider, painfully and minutely, all that part of life which is conspicuously without order; she had had to consider moods and wishes, degrees of liking or disliking, and their effect upon the destiny of people dear to her; she had been forced to deny herself any contemplation of that other part of life where thought constructs a destiny which is independent of human beings [p. 331].

In much the same way Helen Ambrose liked Hirst in *The Voyage Out* because "he took her outside this little world of love and emotion. He had a grasp of facts" (p. 304). Virginia Woolf contrasted domestic life with science again in *A Room of One's Own*. The means by which we ordinarily measure ability, she pointed out, are useless in the home. We know the greatness of Columbus and Newton because they engaged in orders of activity that are governed by known laws. But "there is no mark on the wall to measure the precise height of women. There are no yard measures, neatly divided into the fractions of an inch, that one can lay against the qualities of a good mother or the devotion of a daughter, or the fidelity of a sister" (p. 148). The domestic sphere in the broadest sense, Virginia Woolf implied, circumscribes that part of life that cannot be measured. Logic has no place in the kitchen, the nursery, or the drawing room. Men in Virginia Woolf's novels are able to leave the domestic sphere and enter an impersonal world governed more or less by reason. Women, however, have seldom been able to do so. The contrasting effects of domestic and professional training are illustrated in *Night and Day* by the differences between Ralph Denham, a young solicitor, and his elder sister. "Her face was round but worn, and expressed that tolerant but anxious good humor which is the special attribute of elder sisters in large families. . . . Whereas he seemed to look straightly and keenly at one object, she appeared to be in the habit of considering everything from many different points of view" (p. 29).

Furthermore, domestic life as Virginia Woolf saw it is almost exclusively social; there is no privacy for women. The son of the house may be granted freedom to develop his mind, he may have a room of his own, but the daughter is expected to be at everyone's beck and call. Katharine Hilbery can spare only a few moments a day for the study of mathematics, and those are stolen moments. In *A Room of One's Own* Virginia Woolf ascribed the fact that most women writers have been novelists mainly to their lacking the privacy to write anything that required greater concentration. "The middle-class family in the early nineteenth century was possessed only of a single sitting-room between them. If a woman wrote, she would have to write in the common sitting-room. And, as Miss Nightingale was so vehemently to complain,—'women never have an half hour . . . that they can call their own'—she was always interrupted" (p. 115). Nor was this handicap a thing of the past. "Fiction was, as fiction still is, the easiest thing for a woman to write," she pointed out in "Women and Fiction." "A novel can be taken up or put down more easily than a play or a poem. George Eliot left her work to nurse her father. Charlotte Brontë put down her pen to pick the eyes out of the potatoes."[3]

Katharine Hilbery, as we have seen, experiences a horror of the domestic world ("all that part of life which is conspicuously without order") because her role in it prevents her from exercising her mind. She is starved for abstract ideas, for facts, and shrinks from her emotions; her problem is not that she is lacking in feeling, but that she has too much. For domestic life cultivates the irrational side of a woman's

[3] *Granite and Rainbow*, pp. 78–79.

nature; it is distinguished by the primacy of feeling as science is distinguished by the primacy of intellect. The domestic arts involve, mainly, the fine discrimination of feelings and the ability to bring about adjustments in personal relations. Katharine's mother is a good example of what can happen to a gifted woman when she is confined in the domestic sphere, even under the most favorable circumstances. Mrs. Hilbery is a lovable character; she has a genius for giving parties; her sympathy for the people around her is genuine and her intuitions extremely acute. But her personality is incomplete, one-sided, because she has never had a chance really to develop her mind. She has become eccentric, irrational, and scatterbrained. Although Katharine loves her mother and at times admires her, she does not wish to follow in her footsteps by developing her domestic skills at the expense of her other faculties. For Virginia Woolf, Katharine is the more admirable of the two. Mrs. Hilbery is limited; she is a comic character "beautifully adapted for life in another planet." It is true that Mrs. Hilbery "had a way of seeming the wisest person in the room. But, on the whole, she found it very necessary to seek support in her daughter" (p. 44). Katharine, on the other hand, stands alone. She is struggling to find a place in her life for the life of the mind, to combine her mother's kind of wisdom with more impersonal knowledge. It is this struggle that elevates her and gives her importance in the writer's eyes. The highest achievement, for Virginia Woolf, is the fusion of private or domestic intuitions with general ideas.

Virginia Woolf's feminism, it should be emphasized, implied the broadening, not the rejection, of the domestic wisdom traditionally cultivated by women. Her most poetic books are dotted with homely images drawn from kitchen and nursery. Nor did she attempt, like some feminists, to minimize the difference between the sexes; all her writings stress the fact that men and women are different. She believed, however, that traditional training had drawn the dividing line between them in the wrong place, that women had been excluded arbitrarily from fields of endeavor in which they might excel.

Virginia Woolf tended to think concretely and to visualize ideas like "domestic life" in terms of concrete images. Thus she frequently represented the Victorian family, and occasionally the social structure of which it was the center, by the image of a house. Her use of symbolism is apparent in the case of Katharine Hilbery's house. Ralph Denham, in love with Katharine, comes to look up to her windows at night. The three long windows of the drawing room are lit, and Virginia Woolf likens them to the beams of a lighthouse. Then she continues: "In this little sanctuary were gathered together several different people, but their identity was dissolved in a general glory of something that might, perhaps, be called civilization; at any rate . . . all that stood up above the surge and preserved a consciousness of its own, was centered in the drawing-room of the Hilberys" (p. 395). *Night and Day* celebrates the union of Katharine, who is connected with the intellectual establishment, and Ralph Denham, who comes from an ugly, overcrowded house in the suburbs and represents new life. At the end of the novel, as one reviewer put it, "Highgate has come to Chelsea; raw strength to exquisite tradition."[4] Virginia Woolf, like her father, attributed great importance to domestic life and the influence of women. By means of images like that of the Hilbery drawing room she often identified the feminine domain as the source of civilizing influences.

The image of the house in *The Years*, however, has very different implications. At the beginning of the novel, while the large family is still living there, the Pargiter house seems ample enough; it suggests permanence and stability, not unlike the Hilbery's house, although it lacks the elegance of the latter. But in retrospect, after the family has broken up, it becomes a symbol of the decay of Victorian institutions. Eleanor puts the house up for sale, and in going over it with the young man from the house agents, she sees, through a stranger's eyes, the basement where their old servant had lived for forty years ("she had never realized how dark, how low it was") and feels ashamed. Her brother Martin reflects, "It was an abominable system . . . family life; Abercorn

4   "Night and Day," *TLS*, October 31, 1919, p. 607.

Terrace. No wonder the house would not let. It had one bathroom, and a basement; and there all those different people had lived, boxed up together, telling lies" (pp. 216, 223). The symbolism in the later novel is not made explicit, as it was in *Night and Day*; we simply catch glimpses of the Pargiter house at various times during the story. But unobtrusively Virginia Woolf has associated the fate of the old house with that of the social order whose decline she is chronicling. When Eleanor, riding in a taxi, points out Abercorn Terrace to her niece, the reader finds himself feeling nostalgia for a whole way of life that is gone.

The image of the house plays a still more important part in *To the Lighthouse*. During much of the first section, Mrs. Ramsay sits framed in a window of the Ramsay summer home; the house is her sphere, filled and animated by her influence. It is the shell of the family and Mrs. Ramsay is the life within it. The title of the section, "The Window," is significant. In the second section, "Time Passes," Mrs. Ramsay dies; the house falls into decay. In the final section it is partially restored when some members of the family return, seeking the dead mother.

As in *Night and Day*, the significance of the house is revealed when one of the characters gazes toward its lighted windows. Paul Rayley is returning late from an excursion during which he has become engaged. He sees lights in the distance. "The lights of the town beneath them, the lights coming out suddenly one by one seemed like the things that were going to happen to him—his marriage, his children, his house." Paul reflects that it was Mrs. Ramsay who had given him the courage to propose. Then "turning into the lane that led to the house he could see lights moving about in the upper windows.... People were getting ready for dinner. The house was all lit up, and the lights after the darkness made his eyes feel full, and he said to himself, childishly, as he walked up the drive, lights, lights, lights" (pp. 118, 119). The lights that proclaimed the glory of civilization in *Night and Day* have narrowed their beams here to spell out marriage, children, a home. But these lights are apparently in danger of flickering out, like those in *The Years*. Paul Rayley's marriage is not a happy one; the war breaks out; Mrs. Ramsay dies; other deaths follow. The vacation home, standing unvisited for ten years, is the hero of the second part of *To the Lighthouse*. Mrs. McNab, the cleaning woman, who remembers Mrs. Ramsay as she works to preserve the house, cannot prevent it from falling into ruin. "Now had come that moment, that hesitation when dawn trembles and night pauses, when if a feather alight in the scale it will be weighed down. One feather, and the house, sinking, falling, would have turned and pitched downwards to the depths of darkness. In the ruined room, picnickers would have lit their kettles" (p. 208). But the catastrophe does not take place. Now that the war is over, the family is returning. Orders have been sent to make the house habitable again. The caretakers, working in the dusty corridors, seem to be assisting at "some rusty laborious birth. . . . At last, after days of labor within . . . keys were turned . . . the front door was banged; it was finished" (pp. 210, 212). The final phrase, which may be an echo of the biblical "it is finished," helps put Virginia Woolf's house symbolism into perspective. The same words are repeated twice during the last moments of the book. As Mr. Ramsay completes his symbolic excursion to the lighthouse, Lily Briscoe, painting on the lawn, thinks, "He has landed. . . . It is finished" (p. 309). A moment later she puts the final stroke into the painting in which she has tried to express the harmony created by Mrs. Ramsay, and with that stroke the book comes to an end. "It was done; it was finished. Yes, she thought . . . I have had my vision." These words, "it is finished," link Lily's painting and the landing at the lighthouse to the repairing of Mrs. Ramsay's house. Lily and Mr. Ramsay have found Mrs. Ramsay again. Her house may truly be called a fit dwelling-place for the family now that its indwelling spirit has been restored.

The stability of the house, and of the family—whether or not it can resist decay—is determined by the nature of the spirit that gives it life, the mother. Mrs. Hilbery in *Night and Day* fills her house with light and grace and succeeds in concealing the signs of decay. She lacks the creative power, however, to restore the house to wholeness or to prevent its ultimate ruin. Mrs. Pargiter, in *The Years*, is already ailing as the novel opens, and with her death the Pargiter house crumbles. Mrs. Ramsay's house endures because she abounds in the life-giving power; she is able to create harmony out of the intractable stuff of life. It seems, however, as time passes, that even her power is perishable, that her house will crumble like the others. The last section of *To the Lighthouse* demonstrates that the harmony Mrs. Ramsay has created can survive the passage of time and even her own death.

Mrs. Ramsay creates the family and at the same time embodies a spiritual principle. She not only creates life by giving birth to sons and daughters, she creates meaning by giving harmonious form to their lives in common. Thus, on one level, she is a Great Mother (the portrait is based, after all, on Virginia Woolf's memories of her own mother), but her deliberate shaping of domestic life shows that Mrs. Ramsay is also an artist. The pure mother lives in order to bear children. Virginia Woolf gives us glimpses of her in *The Waves*. Susan lives close to the ground of life.

> The only sayings I understand [she thinks] are cries of love, hate, rage and pain. . . . I shall never have anything but natural happiness. It will almost content me. . . . I shall lie like a field bearing crops in rotation; in the summer heat will dance over me; in the winter I shall be cracked with the cold. . . . My children will carry me on; their teething, their crying, their going to school and coming back will be like the waves of the sea under me [p. 94].

Susan can be contrasted most meaningfully not with Mrs. Ramsay but with a fashionable woman of the world like Clarissa in *Mrs. Dalloway*. Clarissa Dalloway is a hostess with a flair for giving parties, and a natural feeling for society and its conventions. She has a magnetism that draws people to her, but she is conspicuously unsuccessful as a mother. Whereas Susan is so close to the ground of life as almost to lose her individuality, Clarissa is so far removed from it as to lose touch with her basic instincts.[5] Mrs. Ramsay combines

---

5   In order to represent Clarissa's submerged instinctual life, Virginia Woolf created Septimus Smith, her double, who lives as much in the depths as Clarissa does on the surface.

the good qualities of both Susan and Clarissa; she is more complex than either. The life-rhythm flows through her, as it does through Susan, but in her it combines with the overtones of civilization. She equals Clarissa in her accomplishment as a hostess and goes beyond her in elevating social skill to the level of an art. Mrs. Ramsay exists for us as an archetype, and yet Virginia Woolf has succeeded in making her credible as a living human being.

The complex portrait has inspired numerous interpretations. James Hafley sees Mrs. Ramsay as representing the truth of intuition as opposed to the truth of reason. "*To the Lighthouse*," he writes, "is really the story of a contest between two kinds of truth—Mr. Ramsay's and Mrs. Ramsay's. For him, truth is factual truth; for her, truth is the movement toward truth. . . . Mrs. Ramsay . . . knows by intuition rather than by analysis, and is therefore able to know reality."[6] F. L. Overcarsh argues that she is the central figure in an elaborate allegory of the Bible in which she takes the parts of Eve, the Virgin Mary, and Christ.[7] Many other writers identify her, as does J. H. Roberts, with something more general, with "life itself. Without her there is no peace, no completion. It is only by discovering . . . the existence of some inner, unknown force that runs through our lives, that . . . illuminates the conscious with signals flashing from the subconscious as from an unseen lighthouse . . . that humanity solves the mystery of life."[8]

Mrs. Ramsay can be seen clearly only in context, that is, in terms of her relations to her family and friends. Virginia Woolf gives us a sense of her individuality largely through its effects on other people. At the same time, she is making us aware of Mrs. Ramsay's artistry, for the medium in which Mrs. Ramsay exercises her creative powers is social life. The idea that domestic skill of a high order might rank as one of

---

[6]   *The Glass Roof: Virginia Woolf as Novelist* (Berkeley, 1954), p. 82.
[7]   See "The Lighthouse, Face to Face," *Accent* (Winter, 1950), pp. 107-23, especially pp. 109-12.
[8]   "Toward Virginia Woolf," *Virginia Quarterly Review* (October, 1934), pp. 597-98.

the arts had been suggested in Virginia Woolf's earlier novels. In *Night and Day*, for instance, Katharine's management of the Hilbery home had created the impression that "here was an orderly place, shapely, controlled—a place where life had been trained to show to the best advantage, and, though composed of different elements, made to appear harmonious and with a character of its own" (pp. 44-45).[9] In *To the Lighthouse* this idea became central. The dinner party that concludes the first section of the novel is a typical example of Mrs. Ramsay's domestic compositions.

Mrs. Ramsay's dinner party, like her house, comes to seem both real and symbolic. It is one of Mrs. Ramsay's creations; it is also the symbol of her creative powers. She is a lovely woman of flesh and blood, and she is a blind force which terrifies Lily Briscoe, the spinster. The party begins with a group of isolated individuals sitting down, rather dully, to dinner. In the course of the evening a kind of wedding is celebrated by Mrs. Ramsay. She creates a sense of harmony among the ill-assorted guests, and by doing so makes civilized life possible. In her symbolic aspect she appears to represent something more specific than "life itself"; she embodies a particular way of life, a social code, a set of values, usually associated with the Victorians.

The central fact of social relations between men and women, as Virginia Woolf saw them, is that men are socially sterile. Without the harmonizing influence of women there would be no civilization. In *A Room of One's Own* she described the benefit that men seek from women as

---

9   Elsewhere there are suggestions that domestic creativity may give rise to feelings akin to those of religious devotion. Cf. the scene in *Mrs. Dalloway* when Clarissa returns home from shopping for her party: "The hall of the house was cool as a vault. Mrs. Dalloway . . . felt like a nun who has left the world and feels fold round her the familiar veils and the response to old devotions. The cook whistled in the kitchen. She heard the click of the typewriter. It was her life, and, bending her head over the hall table, she bowed beneath the influence, felt blessed and purified" (p. 33).

some stimulus, some renewal of creative power which is in the gift only of the opposite sex to bestow. [A husband] would open the door of drawing-room or nursery . . . and find [his wife] among her children perhaps, or with a piece of embroidery on her knee—at any rate, the centre of some different order and system of life . . . and the sight of her creating in a different medium from his own would so quicken his creative power that insensibly his sterile mind would begin to plot again [pp. 150–51].

Mrs. Ramsay's social code is founded on a tacit recognition of this sterility in men. It is the duty of a woman to cater to men, to smooth the way for them. Her special sympathy for the unattractive Charles Tansley, for instance, is caused by her sense of his inadequacy. "She pitied men," Lily Briscoe thinks, "always as if they lacked something—women never, as if they had something" (p. 129). Under her guidance domestic life is arranged so as to protect the sensitive male ego.

The success of Mrs. Ramsay's dinner party is threatened at first by the egoism of the men. Mr. Ramsay broods; Charles Tansley feels that he is disliked; William Bankes, the scientist, would rather be at home. "Nothing seemed to have merged. They all sat separate. And the whole of the effort of merging and flowing and creating rested on her. Again she felt, as a fact without hostility, the sterility of men, for if she did not do it nobody would do it" (p. 126). Mrs. Ramsay's task is made still more difficult by the antagonism between Charles Tansley and Lily Briscoe. Tansley feels socially inferior, and compensates for it by taunting the lady painter: "Women can't write, women can't paint" (p. 130). Lily's impulse is to retaliate by refusing to perform her part in the contract between men and women, refusing to soothe his injured self-esteem. As a woman, she is instinctively aware of Tansley's extreme discomfort, she is endowed with a sense of social perspective. He, on the other hand, is conscious only of himself. "He wanted somebody to give him a chance of asserting himself." Lily knows perfectly well what the situation, and Mrs. Ramsay, require of her. The code of behavior makes it her duty "to go to the help of the young man opposite so that he may . . . relieve . . . his urgent desire to assert himself; as indeed it is their duty, she reflected . . . to help us, suppose the Tube were to burst into flames. . . . How would it be, she thought, if neither of us did either of these things?" (Pp. 136, 137.) But she catches Mrs. Ramsay's glance from across the table, saying to her, in effect: "Unless you apply some balm to the anguish of this hour and say something nice to that young man there, life will run upon the rocks," and she draws him out in conversation (p. 138). "She had done the usual trick—been nice. She would never know him. He would never know her. Human relations were all like that, she thought, and the worst . . . were between men and women. Inevitably these were extremely insincere" (p. 139).

Insofar as it is coupled with a natural impulse of sympathy, Mrs. Ramsay's social code is good; it smoothes the surface of social relations between men and women and helps to make civilized life possible. The code has a bad effect, however, when it is imposed upon those who no longer believe in it. Then it leads to hypocrisy and ultimately aggravates the antagonisms it is intended to hold in check. Women feel increasingly, as does Lily Briscoe, that they are being placed in false positions. Virginia Woolf observes elsewhere that this insistence that women play a certain social role may have an uglier side still.

Women have served all these centuries as looking-glasses possessing the magic and delicious power of reflecting the figure of man at twice its natural size. Without that power probably the earth would still be swamp and jungle. . . . Mirrors are essential to all violent and heroic action. That is why Napoleon and Mussolini both insist so emphatically upon the inferiority of women, for if they were not inferior, they would cease to enlarge.[10]

There is, perhaps, a hint of Napoleon and Mussolini in Charles Tansley's taunts at Lily. Mrs. Ramsay, however, is able to supply the love in which Lily is lacking, and to reconcile them. It is only years later, after Mrs. Ramsay is dead, that Lily realizes the extent and significance of her achievement.

[10] *A Room of One's Own*, pp. 60–61.

"What a power was in the human soul! she thought. That woman . . . resolved everything into simplicity; made these angers, irritations fall off like old rags; she . . . made out of that miserable silliness and spite (she and Charles squabbling, sparring, had been silly and spiteful) something . . . which survived, after all these years complete . . . and . . . stayed in the mind affecting one almost like a work of art" (pp. 239–40).[11]

Mrs. Ramsay has succeeded, at any rate, in reducing one of the sources of tension between the guests round her table. But her dinner party is still incomplete; two guests are missing without whom she feels unable to compose the harmony of the evening. "Mrs. Ramsay . . . had been uneasy, waiting for Paul and Minta to come in, and unable, she felt, to settle to things. . . They must come now, Mrs. Ramsay thought, look-ing at the door, and at that instant, Minta Doyle, Paul Rayley, and a maid carrying a great dish in her hands came in together" (pp. 147–48). Virginia Woolf probably intended this conjunction of the newly engaged couple with the main dish of the evening to be symbolic. The two young people whom Mrs. Ramsay's skill has brought together do indeed herald the success of her dinner party. For the main dish, Boeuf en Daube, is a masterpiece in its way. It renews William Bankes' waning devotion to his hostess. Then Minta flatters the truculent Mr. Ramsay, as his wife knew she would, and puts him into a good humor. Mrs. Ramsay's three creations, the engagement, the dinner party, and the Boeuf en Daube, are thus linked together. The dinner party has become a sacrificial meal celebrating social union. Paul and Minta are the victims; Mrs. Ramsay is the priestess.

She peered into the dish, with its shiny walls and its confusion of savoury brown and yellow meats and its bay leaves and its wine, and thought, This will celebrate the occasion—a curious

---

[11]   Lily is thinking not so much of the dinner party as of a day at the beach during which Tansley, under the influence of Mrs. Ramsay, had been particularly nice to her. These happy moments were the result of Mrs. Ramsay's sustained creative efforts, of which the dinner party may be considered representative.

The Decline of Family Happiness

sense rising in her, at once freakish and tender, of celebrating a festival. . . .

"It is a triumph," said Mr. Bankes, laying his knife down for a moment [p. 151].

Witnessing Mrs. Ramsay's power Lily Briscoe feels about her almost as one feels about an elemental force: "There was something frightening about her. She was irresistible. Always she got her own way in the end, Lily thought. . . . She put a spell on them all . . . and yet, having brought it all about, somehow laughed, led her victims . . . to the altar" (pp. 152–53). Virginia Woolf intended this marriage to be understood both literally and symbolically. Paul and Minta are young people in love; she has made them into representatives of the race. They are sacrificial victims in the sense that their marriage has been imposed upon them by elemental forces which dwell beyond the realm of individual desires. Mrs. Ramsay, however, now they are engaged, begins at once to scheme to bring Lily and William Bankes together. Helping Bankes to one more piece of meat, peering "into the depths of the earthenware pot," she feels for a moment the harmony she has created, "like a fume rising upwards, holding them safe together. Nothing need be said; nothing could be said. There it was, all around them. It partook, she felt, carefully helping Mr. Bankes to a specially tender piece, of eternity" (p. 158). With the accomplished touch of an artist, Mrs. Ramsay has made the evening which began so trivially yield up a meaning. The dinner has been eaten, has disappeared, but something permanent remains, a creation that partakes "of eternity." On the way upstairs she thinks: "They would . . . however long they lived, come back to this night . . . and to her too. It flattered her, where she was most susceptible of flattery, to think how, wound about in their hearts, however long they lived she would be woven" (p. 170).

Ideally, as Virginia Woolf saw it, the home may at times take on the sanctity of a shrine in which the mother-priestess celebrates a communion, uniting the members of the family circle by means of a mystical life force. The mother must be in touch, like Mrs. Ramsay, both with the conventions of

45

civilized life, and with the primal rhythm that underlies all things; she must be able, somehow, to bridge the gulf between the two.

This ideal domestic harmony can be maintained only by means of a subtle pressure, unrelenting, and almost despotic, in spite of its apparent softness. Disruptive forces in the Ramsay household (the hatred between James and his father is a recurring theme) constantly threaten to destroy what Mrs. Ramsay has created. Here is perhaps the most impressive aspect of Virginia Woolf's achievement in *To the Lighthouse*: by stressing Mrs. Ramsay's artistry, her connection with the primal rhythm, Virginia Woolf has been able to create an ideal mother, who functions on the level of myth, without sacrificing verisimilitude. She has combined novel and poem. We know that the Ramsay household is full of tensions, but we are able to accept the recurring miracles by means of which Mrs. Ramsay frees her loved ones from their own worst instincts; we are able to believe that her influence, continuing after her death, finally reconciles the father and his partially alienated children.

2

When a binding influence such as Mrs. Ramsay's is lacking, real community, and real family life, will be impossible. The evils inherent in the social order will become manifest in the home. As we have seen, Katharine Hilbery, in *Night and Day*, has a horror of family life. Rachel Vinrace, the heroine of Virginia Woolf's first novel, is insulted by a young man at a party and cries out that the sexes "should live separate; we cannot understand each other; we only bring out what's worst."[12] Both young ladies are repelled by the conventional idea of marriage. In these early novels Virginia Woolf pictured the Victorian home as a place of confinement from which her heroines were attempting to escape. Toward the end of her career she described her own struggle to free herself from the phantom of Victorian domesticity.

[12]   *The Voyage Out*, p. 156.

The phantom was a woman, and when I came to know her better I called her after the heroine of a famous poem, The Angel in the House. It was she who used to come between me and my paper when I was writing reviews. It was she who bothered me and wasted my time and so tormented me that at last I killed her. . . . I will describe her as shortly as I can. She was intensely sympathetic. She was immensely charming. She was utterly unselfish. She excelled in the difficult arts of family life. She sacrificed herself daily. If there was chicken, she took the leg; if there was a draught she sat in it—in short she was so constituted that she never had a mind or a wish of her own. . . . Above all—I need not say it—she was pure. . . . In those days— the last of Queen Victoria—every house had its Angel.[13]

Virginia Woolf was in accord with many of her contemporaries in rejecting Victorian values. The social code, she felt, had degenerated in most cases into mere formalism. She regarded Victorian morality as unrealistic and suspected those who professed it of hypocrisy. But she added an article of her own to this condemnation. She believed that most of the evils inherent in Victorian family life could be traced, directly or indirectly, to a single source: the traditional dominance of men. Her views on family life thus were incorporated into the more general scheme of her feminism.

In *The Voyage Out* Virginia Woolf sketched a symbolic portrait of the patriarchy. Evelyn Murgatroyd, who was an illegitimate child, has two photographs of her mother and father mounted in a single frame. When Rachel examines them she notices at once the contrast between the self-assurance of the man and the timidity of the woman. "Mrs. Murgatroyd looked indeed as if the life had been crushed out of her; she knelt on a chair, gazing piteously from behind the body of a Pomeranian dog. . . . The second photograph represented a handsome soldier with high regular features and a heavy black moustache; his hand rested on the hilt of his sword" (p. 250). Evelyn has been cursed from birth as a result of the patriarchal double standard. She dreams of establishing a home for fallen women, but she is too unstable

---

[13]   "Professions for Women," *The Death of the Moth*, pp. 236–37.

even to arrange her own life, and vacillates between rather prosaic lovers. "I'm not anybody in particular," she confides to Rachel. The two photographs ineffectually joined in a single frame represent, for Virginia Woolf, whole ages of English history. A comparable sketch of an unequal couple, this time husband and wife, appears in *Mrs. Dalloway*. In the later novel, however, there is a note of bitterness which was absent from *The Voyage Out*.

Sir William Bradshaw is a fashionable mental specialist to whom Septimus Smith has been taken after threatening to kill himself. Sir William is at the top of his profession; he has got there by dehumanizing himself. The goddess he worships is called Proportion, and the sacrifice she demands is the surrender of one's feelings, blind adherence to convention. The goddess' name reflects ironically on her nature, for she cripples her worshipers by destroying the spontaneity and balance in them that would make them into whole human beings. "Worshipping proportion, Sir William not only prospered himself but made England prosper, secluded her lunatics, forbade childbirth, penalized despair, made it impossible for the unfit to propagate their views until they, too, shared his sense of proportion—his, if they were men, Lady Bradshaw's if they were women" (p. 110). A photograph of Lady Bradshaw in Court dress hangs in the doctor's office. "Fifteen years ago she had gone under. It was nothing you could put your finger on; there had been no scene, no snap; only the slow sinking, water-logged, of her will into his. Sweet was her smile, swift her submission" (p. 111).

The powerful, respected doctor, the pillar of society, is not merely a passive victim of the goddess Proportion; he is himself evil. He is responsible for Septimus Smith's suicide. Septimus is suffering from shellshock. The World War was, for him, the death of human values; Septimus feels that he cannot love, he cannot communicate. Sir William, the healer, should help him to renew his connections with the world around him, he should invoke the power of sympathy that brings people together—but he serves forces that keep them apart. He denies the feelings; he recognizes only the certainties of science and the demands of convention. Sir

William is evil because he is one-sided. In crushing his wife's will he has destroyed a vital part of himself.[14] Septimus glances at the doctor's motor car: "low, powerful, grey with plain initials interlocked on the panel, as if the pomps of heraldry were incongruous, this man being the ghostly helper, the priest of science" (p. 104). The healer, the servant of the spirit, has become an inhuman machine. He has usurped the priest's office but knows nothing of the soul. The social system that honors and advances men like him must be corrupt. Family life modeled upon the union of the Bradshaws, Virginia Woolf implies, is profoundly degrading. Sir William stands for the greatest evil she knows; the unchecked expansion of a single human faculty until it overruns the entire personality and turns a human being into a clockwork puppet. Bradshaw is ruthless in his determination that Septimus shall learn "a sense of proportion" at a sanatorium down in Surrey. "He had to support him police and the good of society, which, he remarked very quietly, would take care, down in Surrey, that these unsocial impulses . . . were held in control. . . . Naked, defenceless, the exhausted, the friendless received the impress of Sir William's will. He swooped; he devoured. He shut people up" (p. 113). Plainly, Sir William is as sick, in his way, as those whom he persecutes. And Septimus, in his terror of a lobotomized life, can see no means of escape from the representatives of the establishment except suicide. Peter Walsh, passing in the street not far from where Septimus has jumped out of the window, hears the bell of an ambulance and reflects, "One of the triumphs of civilization" (p. 166). He is commenting on our collective efficiency and humaneness, but his words, juxtaposed with the image of the sadistic doctor, become an ironic comment on Septimus' death.

This portrait of the patriarch as villain presents an artistic

14 Perhaps this portrait reveals an element of unconscious snobbishness. Sir William is guilty of social climbing. "He had won his position by sheer ability (being the son of a shopkeeper)" (p. 105). The two characters whom Virginia Woolf attacks most vigorously in *Mrs. Dalloway*, Sir William and Miss Kilman, are both of lower-class origin.

problem which Virginia Woolf did not altogether solve until she wrote *The Years*. In reacting against the evils represented by Sir William, she became the victim of her own indignation. She could not resist turning the doctor into a caricature. In the process she emptied him of human qualities—the very thing she had accused him of doing to himself. The result is that *Mrs. Dalloway* is a shallower book than it might have been. Virginia Woolf's doctrinaire attitude caused her to look away from her proper object, "life itself." The inflated language, for instance, in which she describes Lady Bradshaw's subservience to her husband, "this slow sinking, water-logged, of her will into his," reflects an inability to make full contact with the situation. And rhetoric is substituted for dramatic insight in her brief summary of the married life of the Bradshaws: "Quick to minister to the craving which lit her husband's eye so oilily for dominion, for power, she cramped, squeezed, pared, pruned" (p. 112).

The two-dimensionality of Sir William is a flaw, but not a fatal one. For the most part, Virginia Woolf was concerned with the richer life of Clarissa, Septimus, and Peter Walsh. Furthermore, whatever its value as fiction, she did, by means of this portrait, convey a social message of real power. The Bradshaw egoism is typical of the evils of modern life. In the home she saw it taking the form of paternal tyranny; in the mind it was pedantry; in the social code, convention emptied of human values; in politics, dictatorship.

The real sin, then, of the domineering father, is that he infects the other members of the family with his own one-sidedness, and brings the lie into the home. He may have great respect for truth in theory, but like Sir William, he forces others to be untrue to their feelings. The social code, as we have seen in the relationship between Charles Tansley and Lily Briscoe, causes women to be insincere. But the falseness has penetrated deeper still; it has infected the whole institution of marriage. Mrs. Ramsay, for instance, is constantly being forced to propitiate her husband, to soothe his sensitive feelings, to compromise with her own values. Virginia Woolf had described a similarly disquieting situation much earlier, in *The Voyage Out*. What she wrote there, of the Ambroses, holds good of their later counterparts in *To the Lighthouse*.

Terence Hewet, who at times becomes the author's spokesman, reflects about Mr. and Mrs. Ambrose: "She gave way to him; she spoilt him; she arranged things for him; she who was all truth to others was not true to her husband, was not true to her friends if they came in conflict with her husband. It was a strange and piteous flaw in her nature" (p. 242). This marriage, like others with which Terence is acquainted, is a deplorable compromise. "It would have been far better for the world," he concludes, "if these couples had separated." Both Ridley Ambrose and Mr. Ramsay in *To the Lighthouse* are difficult people to live with because, although they are scrupulously accurate about matters of fact, they fail to recognize the truth of the feelings when it comes into conflict with fact. Mrs. Ramsay, who perceives deeper-lying truths, must constantly find ways to circumvent her husband. Her contest with him is epitomized by an argument about the weather that runs through the opening sections of *To the Lighthouse*. Mr. Ramsay forsees that rain will prevent the excursion they have been planning. "The extraordinary irrationality . . . the folly of women's minds enraged him. . . . She flew in the face of facts, made his children hope what was utterly out of the question, in effect, told lies." Mrs. Ramsay, on the other hand, is deeply distressed by her husband's obtuseness. It is more important to her to minimize her little boy James's disappointment than to adhere strictly to the truth. "To pursue truth with such astonishing lack of consideration for other people's feelings, to rend the thin veils of civilization so wantonly, so brutally, was to her . . . an outrage of human decency" (pp. 50, 51). This outrage haunts James for many years; he remembers it much later in the novel, when he and his father finally sail toward the lighthouse. "Something, he remembered, stayed and darkened over him . . . something arid and sharp descended . . . like a blade, a scimitar, smiting through the leaves and flowers. . . . 'It will rain,' he remembered his father saying. 'You won't be able to go to the Lighthouse' " (p. 276).

Virginia Woolf's characterization of Mr. Ramsay, in contrast to her portrayal of Sir William Bradshaw, gained, rather than suffered, as a result of her critical attitude. Perhaps because he was modeled on her own father, she did not fall into the trap of dehumanizing him. In this case, the presence in her mind of a feminist rationale which explained his relationship to the other characters, helped to give greater firmness and credibility to the portrait. As James Hafley has pointed out, two kinds of truth are in conflict in *To the Lighthouse*, and Mrs. Ramsay's domestic truth must give way, at least temporarily, before her husband's facts.[15] But Mr. Ramsay's victory, like Bradshaw's, will in the long run be harmful to him. Another critic sees the falseness in the Ramsay home as the cause of Mrs. Ramsay's death. She "can only submit," he writes, "and repair the damage to the social fabric from her husband's irritability by a pressure of vigilant tactful suggestion under rebuff, which ultimately exhausts her and causes her untimely death."[16] The truth of science, Virginia Woolf believed, must always be balanced by insights that derive from irrational intuitions. When the father imposes purely masculine values in the home he creates a false situation, and contributes to the undermining of family life.

The young lovers in Virginia Woolf's early novels, as I have said, think of marriage as a perpetuation of evils; they are haunted by the Bradshaws. Terence Hewet concludes that it is better to be single than married, especially for a woman. "All the most individual and humane of his friends were bachelors and spinsters; indeed he was surprised to find that the women he most admired and knew best were unmarried women. Marriage seemed to be worse for them than it was for men" (p. 241). And presently he has the thought that "perhaps Rachel had been right . . . when she said . . . 'We bring out what's worst in each other—we should live separate.' " Then Terence reverses himself. "No, Rachel had been utterly wrong! Every argument seemed to be against

---

[15]   See p. 40 above.
[16]   Edwin Berry Burgum, "Virginia Woolf and the Empty Room," *The Novel and the World's Dilemma* (New York, 1947), p. 124.

undertaking the burden of marriage until he came to Rachel's argument, which was manifestly absurd" (p. 242). Virginia Woolf's rejection of the traditional relation between men and women (represented by Bradshaw) necessarily came into conflict with the reverence for family life (Mrs. Ramsay) which was deeply ingrained in her. She viewed marriage from two essentially different points of view, describing it, in an intensely critical spirit, as a patriarchal institution, but also expressing a visionary ideal of marriage as the ultimate relation. Marriage was, for her, irrevocably associated with oppression, but it was also a profound symbol of community.

In the early novels, Virginia Woolf's emphasis was mainly on social evils. Rachel Vinrace and Katharine Hilbery resemble Septimus Smith in an important respect: they cannot communicate, they find it difficult to love. Katharine's alienation is the subject of a key passage in *Night and Day*. Ralph Denham has offered her his friendship. Katharine hesitates. She likes Ralph, but she is afraid of letting down her defences. The conflict leads her to examine her way of life.

As in her thought she was accustomed to complete freedom, why should she perpetually apply so different a standard to her behavior in practice? Why, she reflected, should there be this perpetual disparity between the thought and the action, between the life of solitude and the life of society, this astonishing precipice on one side of which the soul was active and in broad daylight, on the other side of which it was contemplative and dark as night? Was it not possible to step from one to the other, erect, and without essential change? [Pp. 338-39.]

There is a "precipice" separating Katharine's inner life from her life in the world, and *Night and Day*, as the title implies, is about this separation. The conventions which governed her parents' lives are no longer valid for her; she feels that no fruitful inner life can be founded upon them. In order to protect her spark of originality from an indifferent world, she has withdrawn into herself. When Denham brings up the question of how far it is possible to live alone, she answers: "For three weeks I lived entirely by myself, and the only person I spoke to was a stranger in a shop where I lunched. . . .

It doesn't make me out an amiable character, I'm afraid . . .
but I can't endure living with other people" (pp. 334–35). In
agreeing to marry Rodney, a man she doesn't love, Katharine
has accepted her alienation. Denham's offer of friendship is
an attempt to make her reverse that decision. He forces her,
for the first time, to ask herself whether it is not "possible to
step from [solitude to society] erect, and without essential
change." Katharine comes to recognize that an inner life that
is not in relation to the life of the world around her will be
stunted and fruitless. Finally she allows Ralph to persuade her
that it is possible to combine the advantages of solitude with
those of society. The solution he proposes is a somewhat unconventional marriage. They will live together, but each will
have his own work, and, presumably, a room of his own.
The idea of this partnership, as it unfolds in *Night and Day*,
seems like a peculiar hybrid: a cross between romantic love
and a business agreement. A similar ideal is probably half-
formed in Terence Hewet's mind in *The Voyage Out*, when
he dreams of marrying Rachel. "'Oh, you're free!' he ex-
claimed, in exultation . . . 'and I'd keep you free. We'd be
free together'" (p. 244). Equality between the partners must
be accompanied by mutual independence. Denham, in pro-
posing friendship to Katharine, is, in effect, describing his
ideal marriage. "If either [friend] chooses to fall in love, [he
says] he or she does so entirely at his own risk. Neither is under
any obligation to the other. They must be at liberty to break
or to alter at any moment" (p. 337). When Ralph and
Katharine finally, after much hesitation, decide to marry,
neither of them makes any mention of children. Their
marriage is to be an experiment in rational living, an attempt
to reform the relations between men and women. Virginia
Woolf implied in *Night and Day* that such an experiment
might be as important, in its way, as the work of their
suffragist friend, Mary Datchet. The reform of marriage, she
believed, might serve as a means to social regeneration.

Such an idealistic arrangement was, of course, not without
precedent. In her essay on Mary Wollstonecraft, whose
Vindication of the Rights of Women is an early landmark in the
history of English feminism, Virginia Woolf told the story

of an experiment similar to the one proposed by Ralph and Katharine. Virginia Woolf admired Mary Wollstonecraft for heroic efforts to apply the principle of equality in her relations with men, and especially for "that most fruitful experiment, her relation with Godwin." The feminist and the philosopher believed in, and for a time practiced, free love (Katharine and Ralph toy with the idea of living together without marrying), but when Mary became pregnant they decided that it was not "worth while to lose valued friends . . . for the sake of a theory." Another theory, that husband and wife should not live under the same roof, was soon given up as well. They were married, and lived together on terms, which, as Virginia Woolf described them, correspond exactly to the ideals of her fictional couple in *Night and Day*. "Godwin should have a room some doors off to work in; and they should dine out separately if they liked—their work, their friends, should be separate. Thus they settled it, and the plan worked admirably. The arrangement combined 'the novelty and lively sensation of a visit with the more delicious and heart-felt pleasures of domestic life.'" But their marriage had a significance that went beyond the limited sphere of their personal lives. "It too was an experiment," Virginia Woolf wrote, "as Mary's life had been an experiment from the start, an attempt to make human conventions conform more closely to human needs." This problem of the gap between conventions and human needs, so prominent in *Night and Day*, is a recurring theme in Virginia Woolf's works. She concluded her essay on Mary Wollstonecraft by attributing to her a special "form of immortality . . . she is alive and active, she argues and experiments, we hear her voice and trace her influence even now among the living."[17]

[17]   *The Common Reader* (2d ser.), pp. 162, 163. For an account of an
    earlier unconventional marriage, see Virginia Woolf's essay on
    "The Duchess of Newcastle" in *The Common Reader* (1st ser.). Cf.
    the passage on Lady Winchilsea in *A Room of One's Own*, pp.
    101–4. A parallel between Katharine Hilbery and Virginia Woolf
    (both are descended from one of Victorian England's great
    intellectual families, both are rebelling against Victorian institutions)
    suggests that Virginia Woolf may have been drawing upon her

continued at foot of next page

Night and Day ends, before Katharine and Ralph have had a chance to put their plan into effect, ostensibly on a note of optimism. But the final words of the novel, by emphasizing the isolation of these characters, remind us that they may have to overcome inner resistances unknown to Mary Wollstonecraft and Godwin. "She might speak to him, but . . . whom did he answer? What woman did he see? And where was she walking, and who was her companion? . . . From the heart of his darkness he spoke his thanksgiving; from a region as far, as hidden, she answered him" (p. 507). The reader is left wondering whether the lovers have not been fooling themselves. He may suspect, as James Hafley does, that their experiment will have an unhappy ending. "Katharine and Ralph do not at first wish to marry," Hafley writes, "since she has repudiated the social order by breaking her engagement to Rodney; finally, however, and unconvincingly, they see marriage as superficial rather than evil as it concerns them."[18]

The story of Lily Briscoe in *To the Lighthouse* forms an unexpected parallel to that of Katharine Hilbery. Although the two women appear, on the surface, to be very different, their problems are similar. Like Katharine, Lily recoils from the muddle of human relations; she fears the confusion of domestic life and immerses herself in an abstract discipline —her art. Painting, for Lily, is a matter of balancing forms against one another on canvas. The canvas she is working on, and finally finishes, in *To the Lighthouse* represents her attempt to discover a pattern in the irregularity and confusion of the

---

[17] *continued*
> own marriage in sketching the union in *Night and Day*. Her marriage to Leonard Woolf was also a working arrangement, in the sense that her husband accepted the responsibility of being the caretaker of his wife's health and talent, while actively carrying on a career of his own as a social critic and editor. Virginia Woolf's attitude toward her husband, described by Aileen Pippett as "admiration (amounting, observers said, almost to awe at times) of his abilities and devotion to public affairs" is similar to Katharine's attitude toward Ralph Denham. See *The Moth and the Star: A Biography of Virginia Woolf* (Boston, 1955), p. 81.

[18]   *The Glass Roof*, p. 29.

Ramsay household, and to give it permanent expression in art. By doing so she places herself above, or beyond, that confusion; it seems clear that she is destined to become an old maid. Mrs. Ramsay, however, would like Lily to marry William Bankes, the botanist, even though Bankes seems to care not for Lily but for Mrs. Ramsay herself. "Oh, but nonsense, she thought; William must marry Lily. They have so many things in common. Lily is so fond of flowers. They are both cold and aloof and rather self-sufficing" (p. 157). One can imagine an arrangement between them similar to Ralph and Katharine's; they might live together in mutual respect, childless, each doing his own work. But here there is none of the romance which Virginia Woolf created between the lovers in *Night and Day*. Lily completely lacks Katharine's beauty and mystery; she is small and unattractive. Nor does William Bankes have any of the impetuousness and idealism that make Ralph Denham attractive; he is a middle-aged man, set in his ways. Although she sincerely likes Bankes, Lily resists Mrs. Ramsay's urging. The impersonal world which she inhabits as an artist is incompatible, she feels, with marriage, even to William Bankes. The decision never to marry is linked in her mind with a decision to revise the composition of the painting she has been working on by changing the position of a tree. Revisiting the Ramsays years after her chance of marriage has passed, she reflects that "she had only escaped by the skin of her teeth. . . . She had been looking at the table-cloth, and it had flashed upon her that she would move the tree to the middle, and need never marry anybody, and she had felt an enormous exultation" (p. 262). The painting, as we have said, is Lily's expression of the harmony Mrs. Ramsay has made her feel; it is the pattern she has found in family life. Her decision to change the painting corresponds to the social changes of which her life is an example. *Because* she has moved the tree to the middle, and changed the pattern, Lily need not marry.

In spite of Lily's decision, Katharine and Ralph's experiment does have its counterpart in *To the Lighthouse*. In the later book it appears, shorn of romantic elements, in the form of the enduring and disinterested friendship that has sprung up between Lily and William Bankes. This friendship, based upon a combination of deep sympathy and strict reserve, is more than a casual relationship. It is a form of love. Perhaps these two people have come as close as is humanly possible to Terence Hewet's ideal of being "free together." Lily reflects gratefully that she can talk to William Bankes about what is dearest to her—her painting. "Thanks to his scientific mind he understood—a proof of disinterested intelligence which had pleased her and comforted her enormously. One could talk of painting then seriously to a man. Indeed, his friendship had been one of the pleasures of her life. She loved William Bankes" (pp. 262–63). Like the lovers in *Night and Day*, Lily and William Bankes are unable to accept some of the values that Mrs. Ramsay holds dearest. They must fashion their lives according to patterns unknown to her.

The idea that there are varieties of love between men and women which cannot be contained within the confines of married life is strikingly illustrated in *The Years*. Sara and Nicholas, close friends for many years, have never married because Nicholas is a homosexual; but they love each other. Eleanor Pargiter meets them together during the party at the end of the novel. Nicholas is affectionately teasing Sara:

"... coming to a party," he was saying, "with one stocking that is white, and one stocking that is blue". . . . This is their love-making, Eleanor thought, half listening to their laughter, to their bickering. . . . And if this love-making differs from the old, still it has its charm; it was "love," different from the old love, perhaps, but worse, was it? Anyhow, she thought, they are aware of each other; they live in each other; what else is love, she asked. . . . But they are very happy. . . . They laugh at each other [p. 370].

It would have been impossible for Virginia Woolf to describe relations between a man and woman in these terms in an early novel like *Night and Day*. But Sara and Nicholas resemble Katharine and Ralph in attempting "to make human conventions conform more closely to human needs." The old modes of family life are dying; people are casting about in the void and creating new social forms. In a sense, Virginia Woolf's fictional technique kept pace with the changing customs she was describing. As a modern novelist she emphasized the fragmentation of experience, the relativity of values. She sought a combination of the old and new (witness *The Years*), just as the characters in her stories attempt to give new content to traditional social forms. In her prose style itself she combined stately traditional rhythms and more personal modes of expression. She was in a dynamic relation to tradition. When she swung too far away from it, the influence of her early training made her swing back, until the necessities of her subject matter reversed the process once again. Thus her feminism, and her traditionalism may be thought of as regulators, the one on her aesthetic sensibilities, the other on her inclination to experiment.

Virginia Woolf had mixed feelings about many of the social changes that were taking place, just as she had mixed feelings about the Victorian institutions. *To the Lighthouse* had combined veneration and hatred; nostalgia and disgust. As a feminist, Virginia Woolf wished to clear away the debris of the past, even though it might mean tearing up her own roots. But her desire for reform was accompanied by a sense of loss. The simplicity and natural happiness which one could still find among the "unconcerned, contented, indifferent middle classes of England" was lost to her and her intellectual friends forever, and was disappearing everywhere. In 1926 she described finding this happiness "at a family party of an English banker, where the passion and joy of sons and daughters in their own society struck me almost to tears with self-pity and amazement. Nothing of that sort do we any of us know—profound emotions, which are yet natural and taken for granted, so that nothing inhibits or restrains." She borrowed a parable from *Father and Son*, by Edmond Gosse. In the nineteenth century, it went, "all the coast of England was fringed with little sea anemones and lovely tassels of seaweed and sprays of emerald moss, [but] for some reason hordes of clergy and spinsters" began rifling the coast until this treasure was destroyed for ever. "A parable, this, of what we have done to the deposits of family happiness."[19]

---

[19] Quoted by Pippett in *The Moth and the Star*, pp. 219-20.

The Decline of Family Happiness

The Years was completed about ten years after she wrote these words. In this late novel Virginia Woolf begins by showing that the old family happiness has passed away; it was killed by the Victorians. Does anything, then, remain to celebrate, she seems to be asking as she gathers her characters together at Delia's party. Yes, we must see marriage from a new perspective—or a very ancient one—as ultimate relationship. Perhaps the tie that binds Sarah and Nicholas, for example, should also be called "marriage," although there can be no room in it for family life?

The brief scene that follows Eleanor's meeting with these two friends at the party dramatizes Virginia Woolf's contrasting views of marriage. Eleanor's nephew, North, has come up, and watches Sara and Nicholas, who have begun to dance. North has just made a date with a pretty girl, and is elated. "Everybody ought to marry," he remarks to his Aunt Eleanor, who is a spinster. Across the room he sees a young couple gazing at each other, united by some powerful emotion.

As he looked at them, some emotion about himself, about his own life, came over him, and he arranged another background for them or for himself—not the mantelpiece and the bookcase, but cataracts roaring, clouds racing, and they stood on a cliff above a torrent. . . .
"Marriage isn't for everyone," Eleanor interrupted.
He started. "No. Of course not," he agreed. He looked at her. She had never married. Why not? he wondered. Sacrificed to the family, he supposed—old Grandpapa without any fingers [p. 372].

Insofar as marriage is rooted in patriarchal institutions still dominated by "old Grandpapa without any fingers," Virginia Woolf believed that it is evil. But she imagined marriage free of such conditions as the ultimate relationship—two people facing each other "on a cliff above a torrent." Marriage in this ideal sense exists independently of social or historical accidents; it is a function of the human soul. Virginia Woolf used this idea as a fixed point of reference in both her last novels.

In *The Years* the ideal relation of man and woman is represented by an image of a couple riding in a taxicab. This image

60

had appeared previously in *A Room of One's Own*, where
Virginia Woolf had used it to suggest the need for a balance
of masculine and feminine elements in the human mind. The
image may in part retain this implication in *The Years*, but
the emphasis has been changed and the meaning extended.
At the beginning of the novel, in 1880, the Pargiter girls are
sitting in their drawing room at dusk; their mother is lying,
upstairs, dying. Eleanor's sister, Delia, who has been peeking
into the street, notices a hansom cab approaching and thinks
for a moment that someone is coming to call, but the cab
stops at a neighbor's door; a young man wearing a top hat
descends. She stands staring into the empty street.

> Dropping the blind, Delia turned, and coming back into the
> drawing-room, said suddenly:
> "Oh, my God!"
> Eleanor, who had taken her books again, looked up disturbed.
> "Eight times eight . . ." she said aloud. "What's eight times
> eight?"
> Putting her finger on the page to mark the place, she looked
> at her sister. . . .
> "Look here, Delia," said Eleanor . . . "you've only got to
> wait . . ." She meant but she could not say it, "until Mama dies."
> "No, no, no," said Delia. . . . "It's hopeless" [pp. 19–20].

Fifty years later, in a scene that is thematically linked to this
one, old Eleanor rides in a taxi with her niece Peggy. Peggy
is a young doctor who regards her aunt as a fascinating relic
of an almost legendary era. She imagines the way in which
she will describe Eleanor to a friend at the hospital where she
works. "The things she wants explained," she will say, "are
either as simple as two and two make four, or so difficult that
nobody in the world knows the answer. And if you say to
her, 'What's eight times eight? . . .' " But before she can complete her thought Eleanor interrupts her (p. 334). The recur-
rence of this bit of simple arithmetic establishes, for the first
time, the connection to the earlier scene. A little later, Peggy
notices that Eleanor is attracted by the bright clothes that
someone in the street is wearing.

> Anything distracts Eleanor, everything interests her, she
> thought.

"Was it that you were suppressed when you were young?"
she said aloud, recalling vaguely some childish memory; her
grandfather with the shiny stumps instead of fingers; and a long
dark drawing-room. Eleanor turned. She was surprised.

"Suppressed?" she repeated. She so seldom thought about
herself now that she was surprised.

"Oh, I see what you mean," she added after a moment. A
picture . . . had swum to the surface. There was Delia standing
in the middle of the room; Oh, my God! Oh, my God! she was
saying; a hansom cab had stopped at the house next door [p. 335].

Delia has long since married; it is her party to which they
are driving. The incident of the hansom cab, with the frustration it implies, seems to relate more directly to Eleanor's
life than to Delia's. It was she, quietly keeping the household
books, whose chance of an independent life was sacrificed to
family considerations. Eleanor is a pathetic—in a way, a
heroic—character. She recognizes the man she might have
loved twenty years too late. Her most important statements
are always interrupted. She submits. Nevertheless, she retains
her inherent dignity. But the slight incident of the cab suggests a lifetime of suppression and unfulfilment.

Manifold threads, stretching from the past into the present,
are drawn together at Delia's party, which lasts till dawn. And
at dawn, Eleanor has the vision which, for Virginia Woolf,
solves the riddle of the passing years, and ends the book.
Eleanor is looking out the window as the guests depart. The
sun has just risen. "She was watching a taxi that was gliding
slowly round the square. It stopped in front of a house two
doors down." Then Delia interrupts by calling to Eleanor,
her arms full of flowers.

But she was watching the cab. A young man had got out; he
paid the driver. Then a girl in a tweed travelling suit followed
him. He fitted his latch-key to the door. "There," Eleanor
murmured, as he opened the door and they stood for a moment
on the threshold, "There!" she repeated as the door shut with a
little thud behind them.

Then she turned round into the room. "And now?" she said,
looking at Morris [her brother] who was drinking the last drops
of a glass of wine. "And now?" she asked, holding out her
hands to him.

And the book ends with a brief impression of early morning like a benediction: "The sun had risen, and the sky above the houses wore an air of extraordinary beauty, simplicity and peace." The beauty of the new day, the freshness of nature, the flowers, suggest the hope that a renewal may be possible on the human plane as well. Like the sun and the sky, the fundamental human relations have not lost their freshness. That is the vision, simple and profound, that Eleanor has at the window, watching the couple who may be starting a new life together. "The two who drove off in the taxi in *A Room of One's Own* have come home."[20]

In her last novel, *Between the Acts*, Virginia Woolf used another image—that of the two figures against the sky, which had appeared fleetingly in *The Years*—to express her vision of marriage and to link it to the primitive instincts which are a part of the human inheritance. Isa and Giles Oliver live in the big house where a pageant of English history, written by Miss La Trobe, is being presented by the villagers. Giles is full of repressed violence; he rages against the uselessness of his life as a stockbroker in the City. Isa, in her turn, has been casting adulterous glances at a neighboring gentleman farmer. Looking at her husband, she thinks, " 'The father of my children, whom I love and hate.' Love and hate—how they tore her asunder!" (P. 215.) Their marriage, with its adulterous impulses, its much reduced family circle, its general atmosphere of dissatisfaction, seems many generations distant from the stately family life of the Ramsays.

Miss La Trobe, the lesbian writer, has been struggling to discover a pattern in the confusion she sees around her. At the end of *Between the Acts* she begins to interpret the relationship of the Olivers in terms of her art, as Lily Briscoe interpreted the family life of the Ramsays in *To the Lighthouse*. She is packing up after the pageant, which has just been given, when she has a vision of a new work. " 'I should group them,' she murmured, 'here.' It would be midnight; there would be two figures, half concealed by a rock. The curtain would

---

[20]   Dorothy Brewster, *Virginia Woolf's London* (New York, 1960), p. 111.

rise. What would the first words be? The words escaped her" (p. 210). Later, drinking alone in a pud, the vision appears to her once again, more clearly. "There was the high ground at midnight; there the rock; and two scarcely perceptible figures. . . . She set down her glass. She heard the first words" (p. 212). As the book ends, Virginia Woolf shows us Isa and Giles, transformed into Miss La Trobe's archetypal figures, beginning to act out the universal drama which she, in a sense, has conceived for them. It is late at night, and they are sitting in the drawing room.

> Left alone together for the first time that day, they were silent. Alone, enmity was bared; also love. Before they slept, they must fight; after they had fought, they would embrace. From that embrace another life might be born. . . .
> Isa let her sewing drop. The great hooded chairs had become enormous. And Giles too. And Isa too against the window. The window was all sky without colour. The house had lost its shelter. It was night before roads were made, or houses. It was the night that dwellers in caves had watched from some high place among rocks.
> Then the curtain rose. They spoke.

In *The Years* and *Between the Acts* Virginia Woolf implied that the truth about human relations can no longer be expressed in terms of social institutions, such as marriage and the family. It must be expressed in racial terms, in mythical terms. The individual is more isolated than ever before because he cannot come in under an umbrella of common social forms, and thus escape from his sense of isolation. The last line of retreat left open to him is an emphasis upon what all people have in common, merely by virtue of their humanity. This emphasis is found in both of Virginia Woolf's last novels. In describing the disintegration of the old order, while, at the same time, pointing out universal patterns within the apparent chaos, her work is parallel to that of Joyce. The figures of the two lovers silhouetted against the sky reveal the univeral in the particular, as Joyce's prosaic Leopold Bloom reveals the archetypal Ulysses.

··◦[3]◦··

The Sins of the Fathers

I

The decline of family happiness, Virginia Woolf observed, was directly linked to disturbing events that were taking place in public life. "The public and the private worlds are inseparably connected," she wrote in *Three Guineas*; "the tyrannies and servilities of the one are the tyrannies and servilities of the other." Discussing the question of how war might be prevented, she devoted many pages to the oppression of women, in both private and public life, because she saw both phenomena as part of a single chain of causes and effects all tending toward the same evil. Fear, she said, destroys freedom in the private house. "That fear, small, insignificant and private as it is, is connected with the other fear, the public fear," which leads people to go to war (pp. 257, 258). Petty domestic tyranny paves the way for public dictatorship. Private wrongs are the foundations upon which social injustice is built. Most of Virginia Woolf's discussions of family life and the social code, accordingly, merge almost imperceptibly with comments about the patriarchy and the status of women.

During the greater part of English history women had been little better than slaves; they had been "locked up, beaten and flung about the room." So Virginia Woolf concluded in *A Room of One's Own* (p. 75), having consulted Trevelyan's *History of England*. There she had read that for hundreds of years women had lacked the freedom to choose their husbands, that they had been married almost before they were out of the nursery, and that the new husband had been "lord and master, so far at least as law and custom could make him" (p. 73). Joining this image with the image of woman found in literature, she had pointed out an anomaly: woman dominated "the lives of kings and conquerors in fiction; in fact she was the slave of any boy whose parents forced a ring upon her finger. Some of the most inspired words . . . in literature fall from her lips; in real life she . . . could scarcely spell, and was the property of her husband" (p. 75). Virginia Woolf saw the double image as a strange monster, "the spirit of life and beauty in a kitchen chopping up suet" (p. 76). The fictional image had governed the imaginations of men, but it was the image of the illiterate drudge that stood closest to reality. According to Virginia Woolf, women in twentieth-century England were still accorded the same flattery and hampered by the same restrictions which had made virtual slaves of them in the past. One might find evidence in any newspaper, she pointed out, unmistakable evidence "that England is under the rule of a patriarchy." She had previously drawn a picture of a misogynist professor whose monumental work was entitled *The Mental, Moral, and Physical Inferiority of the Female Sex*. "He was not in my picture a man attractive to women. He was heavily built; he had a great jowl; to balance that he had very small eyes; he was very red in the face" (p. 52). And now, consulting the evidence of the newspaper, she found him in power everywhere. "Nobody in their senses could fail to detect the dominance of the professor. His was the power and the money and the influence.[1] He was the proprietor of the

---

[1] The biblical echo is significant; Virginia Woolf associated traditional religion with patriarchal tyranny.

paper and its editor. . . . He was the Foreign Secretary and the Judge. . . . He was the director of the company that pays two hundred per cent to its shareholders. He left millions to charities and colleges. . . . With the exception of the fog he seemed to control everything" (p. 57). English society had been made by and for men, and it was an inescapable corollary that the evils of competitiveness, avarice, and war, were also the creations of men. Women had no status, no power, Virginia Woolf concluded in *Three Guineas*. In order to keep this reality uppermost in the minds of her readers she began referring to middle-class women as "outsiders." It was her contention that an outsider has a far smaller stake in her country than the average man, and elaborating on this view she pictured a patriotic man trying to convince a woman of the need for war. The woman, she advised, should consider critically what the appeal to patriotism and the words "our country" mean to her:

She will inform herself of the position of her sex and her class in the past. She will inform herself of the amount of land, wealth and property in the possession of her own sex and class in the present—how much of "England" in fact belongs to her. From the same sources she will inform herself of the legal protection which the law has given her in the past and now gives her. . . . All these facts will convince her reason . . . that her sex and class has very little to thank England for in the past; not much to thank England for in the present; while the security of her person in the future is highly dubious.[2]

These remarks are severe, but by no means untypical. For an indication of how consistent Virginia Woolf was in her feminist nonconformism we need only turn to her first novel, *The Voyage Out*, and consider the radical views of Helen Ambrose, a character with whom the author clearly sympathizes. "Helen remarked that it seemed to her as wrong to keep sailors as to keep a Zoo, and that as for dying on a battle-field, surely it was time we ceased to praise courage" (p. 69). Helen's attitude toward religion proves to be equally unconventional. Talking of the education of her children she

[2] *Three Guineas*, pp. 195–96.

boasts that "so far, owing to great care on my part, they think of God as a kind of walrus" (p. 27). Her remarks have all the more point because they are addressed to men whom she has criticized in her mind for their one-sidedness, their lack of feminine subtlety. Nor is Helen Ambrose the only character in *The Voyage Out* who appears to express the author's feminist views. Terence Hewet seems at times to be little more than a mouthpiece. The young aspiring novelist is especially interested, we are told, in the prosaic day-to-day lives of women, the portion of experience that has never yet been recorded. This is a subject that fascinated Virginia Woolf, but she was not altogether convincing when she attributed the same interest to a young man. Terence gets Rachel to describe in detail an average day at Richmond, the suburb where she had been brought up by two maiden aunts. And from meditating on the conventional monotony of this existence Terence's thoughts turn to the lives of the great anonymous mass of women. " 'I've often walked along the streets where people live all in a row, and one house is exactly like another house, and wondered what on earth the women were doing inside,' he mused. 'Doesn't it make your blood boil?' he asked suddenly. . . . 'I'm sure if I were a woman I'd blow someone's brains out' " (p. 215). It is no very great step from these sentiments to the indignant assertion in *Three Guineas* that women have "very little to thank England for in the past; not much to thank England for in the present."

These passages are fair examples of what E. M. Forster calls Virginia Woolf's "extreme feminism." She rarely, in any of her writings, voiced a social or political opinion that was not in some way connected with feminism. She observed the life around her with the keen but selective vision of the lyric poet; and one of the areas that fell within the intense circle of her vision was the daily life of women. She was interested in anything that could extend her knowledge of her sex, although she realized that she would never fully understand women outside her own social class. A detailed record of her observations of the lives of women can be traced in her novels. Furthermore, she read everything by and about women that she could lay her hands on. The results of her research into the women's movement and related subjects were incorporated into her feminist tracts. To a great extent her conclusion had already been formed at the outset. It was not very difficult to find evidence to strengthen her conviction that women were victims of oppression. She measured every phase of life, every social convention, with the same yardstick; almost all were found wanting. In *A Room of One's Own* and *Three Guineas* she presented a catalogue of grievances, an anatomy of the sins of the fathers.

The social injustices against which Virginia Woolf protested may be placed under two headings. On the one hand were prohibitions which prevented women from developing intellectually and spiritually—which, in the broadest sense, interfered with their education. On the other hand were restrictions which limited them materially, that is, prevented them from acquiring too much money or power. The titles of her two long essays on feminism contain suggestions of these categories. *A Room of One's Own* refers not merely to the need for privacy but to the freedom to seek experience and to cultivate the mind. *Three Guineas* of course suggests the need for economic independence.

Virginia Woolf was particularly conscious of the prohibitions that checked the intellectual growth of women. Clive Bell feels that "what she minded most, perhaps, was what she considered male advantages, and especially advantages in education."[3] As a novelist, there were many things that she wanted to know and would never be able to know from first-hand experience because she was a woman. As an intellectual, she coveted the rigorous university education, the cultivation of mind, which was still beyond the reach of most women. In her essays on women writers of the past she repeatedly stresses the fact that, in order to acquire a little knowledge of the world, they had to surmount numerous obstacles put in their way by a hostile society. Charlotte Brontë, a woman of genius, had been cramped and thwarted by being shut away in the country. She had longed for the opportunity to know

3   "Virginia Woolf," *Old Friends* (London, 1956), p. 101.

more "of the busy world, towns, regions full of life." In *A Room of One's Own*, Virginia Woolf quoted a bitter passage from *Jane Eyre*: "Millions are condemned to a stiller doom than mine, and millions are in silent revolt against their lot. Nobody knows how many rebellions ferment in the masses of life which people earth. Women are supposed to be very calm generally: but women feel just as men feel" (p. 119). And the indignation which had burst forth from Charlotte Brontë in *Jane Eyre* caused an awkward break in the novel. She would never, because of that irritation, "get her genius expressed whole and entire." Charlotte Brontë knew very well, Virginia Woolf added, "how enormously her genius would have profited if it had not spent itself in solitary visions over distant fields; if experience and intercourse and travel had been granted her" (pp. 120, 121).

George Eliot, another woman of genius, broke out of the prison of convention by going to live with G. H. Lewes without being married to him; but, having done so, she shut herself up, voluntarily, in a narrower prison still, living the isolated life of the semi-outcast. "I wish it to be understood," she wrote, "that I should never invite any one to come and see me who did not ask for the invitation."[4]

Virginia Woolf pointed the moral:

> At the same time, on the other side of Europe, there was a young man living freely with this gipsy or with that great lady; going to the wars; picking up unhindered and uncensored all that varied experience of human life which served him so splendidly later when he came to write his books. Had Tolstoi lived at the Priory in seclusion with a married lady "cut off from what is called the world," however edifying the moral lesson, he could scarcely, I thought, have written *War and Peace* [pp. 122–23].

Virginia Woolf felt these deprivations keenly on her own account. In *Orlando* she wrote of a hero-heroine "living freely with this gipsy or with that great lady," rather like the young Tolstoi; his exploits were described with obvious relish. It seems likely that the hectic freedom of the young bachelor's

---

4   Quoted in *A Room of One's Own*, p. 122.

life appealed strongly to some part of her nature. *Orlando*
gave her an opportunity, if only vicariously, to extend her
experience beyond the limits usually ordained for her sex and
class. Writing of amorous intrigues—varied by several
changes of sex—permitted her, in a sense, to revel in freedom.
It was a kind of freedom unknown to the nineteenth-century
women novelists whom she was discussing in *A Room of One's
Own* at about the same time that she was writing her fantasy
novel. In "Women and Fiction" she asserted that *"Pride and
Prejudice, Wuthering Heights, Villette,* and *Middlemarch* were
written by women from whom was forcibly withheld all
experience save that which could be met with in a middle-
class drawing-room."[5] Virginia Woolf meant this statement
literally; had she not repeatedly reminded her readers that it
was improper for a middle-class young woman in the nineteenth century to go about alone? There was the example of
Gertrude Bell, "who, though the diplomatic service was and
is shut to women, occupied a post in the East which almost
entitled her to be called a pseudo-diplomat—we find rather
to our surprise that 'Gertrude could never go out in London
without a female friend or, failing that, a maid.'" And there
was the typical complaint of another "educated man's
daughter": "How many a long dull summer's day have I
passed immured indoors because there was no room for me
in the family carriage and no lady's maid who had time to
walk out with me."[6] How much knowledge of the world
could this young woman acquire? Even in the country the
young lady's movements were so much impeded by the
clothes she wore that she could not enjoy the freedom of the
fields. Orlando found, when, in the course of her long life,
she arrived in the nineteenth century, that the dress then in
fashion was drabber and heavier than that of any previous age
she had known. "No longer could she stride through the
garden with her dogs, or run lightly to the high mound and
fling herself beneath the oak tree. Her skirts collected damp
leaves and straw. The plumed hat tossed on the breeze. The

---

5   In *Granite and Rainbow*, p. 79.
6   *Three Guineas*, pp. 139, 68.

thin shoes were quickly soaked and mudcaked" (pp. 244-45). The historical fantasy of *Orlando* reminds us that Virginia Woolf was acutely sensitive to the influence of the past. Frequently, in describing the way of life that had been so oppressive to women in the preceding century, she seemed to be protesting these grievances of the past as if they were her own. The sufferings of Charlotte Brontë and George Eliot were not dead facts to her, but living problems. The effect of this attitude is to make it seem, occasionally, that the scope of the present has been extended, that contemporaneity has been shifted back to include a great part of the nineteenth century. Virginia Woolf was not only deeply rooted in the previous century, but, like many members of her class, she seemed at times unable fully to comprehend that a new age had dawned. Rarely did she mark a dividing line between those grievances that were essentially things of the past, and those that still troubled her own time. Her purpose was to expose abuses, not to mark the progress that had been made toward eliminating them.

Looking at the education of young women in the nineteenth century, she observed that it was in keeping with the rest of their experience. It was designed to teach them to cope with no more of life than "could be met with in a middle-class drawing-room." There was no such thing as higher education for women till the latter years of Victoria's reign; and on lower levels, the formal education provided for girls was inferior to that of their brothers because their education was thought of as a dead-end street that led them back to domestic life. But, for the most part, women had to rely on the informal education of the private house, and on what Virginia Woolf called the "unpaid-for education." The two were not quite identical.

Here is Virginia Woolf's description of the education of a well-to-do girl in the last part of the nineteenth century:

> Kindly doctors and gentle old professors had taught her the rudiments of about ten different branches of knowledge, but they would as soon have forced her to go through one piece of drudgery thoroughly as they would have told her that her hands were dirty. . . . There was no subject in the world which she

knew accurately. Her mind was in the state of an intelligent man's in the beginning of the reign of Queen Elizabeth; she would believe practically anything she was told, invent reasons for anything she said.[7]

A glance at Virginia Woolf's essay on Elizabeth Barrett Browning's "Aurora Leigh" helps to round out the picture. In addition to the more academic part of her studies ("a little French, a little algebra; the internal laws of the Burmese empire; what navigable river joins itself to Lara; what census of the year five was taken at Klagenfurt"), the well-to-do girl also learned "how to draw nereids neatly draped, to spin glass, to stuff birds and model flowers in wax. . . . Of an evening she did cross-stitch. . . . Under this torture of women's education . . . certain women have died; others pine. . . ."[8] The final goal of this education of the private house, as everyone knows, was marriage. There was really no intention of improving the young lady's understanding —simply a desire to make and keep her a saleable commodity on the marriage market. She was therefore not only to be taught certain accomplishments, but to be zealously prevented from becoming adept at anything, for this would lesson her desirability as a wife. It was therefore that "she tinkled on the piano, but was not allowed to join an orchestra; sketched innocent domestic scenes, but was not allowed to study from the nude. . . . The streets were shut to her . . . the fields were shut to her . . . solitude was denied her . . . in order that she might preserve her body intact for her husband."[9]

The inferiority of the daughter's education was all the greater because of the large sums required for educating the son. Sisters have always sacrificed themselves in order to provide opportunities for their brothers. For hundreds of years, Virginia Woolf complained, money that might have been distributed among all the children had been set aside for the sole use of the males. Twenty to thirty pounds were spent on Mary Kingsley's education, she tells us, two thousand on

---

[7] *The Voyage Out*, pp. 33–34.
[8] *The Common Reader* (2d ser.), pp. 204–5.
[9] *Three Guineas*, p. 70.

her brother's.[10] The resulting inequality was responsible for the difficulty which men and women found in communicating. They appeared to speak the same language, but in fact they were as far apart as hundreds of years of privilege on the one hand, and of neglect on the other, could make them.

> What is that congregation of buildings there, with a semi-monastic look, with chapels and halls and green playing-fields? To you it is your old school; Eton or Harrow; your old university, Oxford or Cambridge; the source of memories and of traditions innumerable. But to us . . . it is a schoolroom table; an omnibus going to a class; a little woman with a red nose who is not well educated herself but has an invalid mother to support.[11]

Being deprived of opportunity and enjoyment, having to learn to abstain, constitutes a kind of education in itself. It was in reference to this system of negative pedagogy that Virginia Woolf coined the term "unpaid-for education." She had learned something about the "unpaid-for education" by consulting the biographies of famous women: Florence Nightingale, Miss Clough, Mary Kingsley, Gertrude Bell. They had all been educated by the same teachers, "poverty, chastity, derision, and . . . freedom from unreal loyalties," she said in *Three Guineas* (p. 142). It had been a bitter discipline, not entirely without virtues, as the moral character and accomplishments of these women seemed to prove, but it had inspired them in the end with so passionate a hatred that they had determined to "undertake any task however menial, exercise any fascination however fatal" in order to escape (p. 72). Florence Nightingale greeted the Crimean War with "natural delight" because it permitted her to escape. During World War I, Virginia Woolf said, masses of women had followed Miss Nightingale's example, refugees flying from the "horrors" of the "unpaid-for education" to the "comparative amenity" of hospitals, harvest fields and munition works (p. 143).

But most women were not so lucky as to have the pretext

10 See *ibid.*, pp. 9–13, 263.
11 *Ibid.*, p. 11.

of a war for evading their "unpaid-for education." The avenue of escape in normal times was still very narrow. The women's colleges held out a hope, but they were so poor that they could not fully perform their function. The professions were now open, but rarely could a woman advance very far in them. The restrictions which had always prevented women from acquiring money and power were still in force. Virginia Woolf protested that they made freedom impossible; they stood in the way of growth.

The poverty of women was an important item in her indictment. "A woman must have money and a room of her own if she is to write fiction." This statement was the starting-point of *A Room of One's Own*. Formed into a question— Why are women poor?—it brought her, in search of an answer, to the British Museum, where under the heading "Women and Poverty" she assembled a list of references ranging from "Condition in Middle Ages of" to "Dr. Johnson's opinion of." She had already recorded the obvious answer to her question: "It is only for the last forty-eight years that Mrs. Seton [who represents the Victorian wife and mother] has had a penny of her own. For all the centuries before that it would have been her husband's property—a thought which, perhaps, may have had its share in keeping Mrs. Seton . . . off the Stock Exchange. Every penny I earn, [she] may have said, will be taken from me and disposed of according to my husband's wisdom" (p. 38). But this answer did not entirely satisfy Virginia Woolf; she kept pressing the inquiry.[12] It seems that, in accordance with one of the habits of her mind, a whole range of grievances had become crystallized for her in the idea of money, and that she was making the term "poverty" mean something more general

[12] The poverty of women is one of Virginia Woolf's main themes in *Three Guineas*—as in *A Room of One's Own*. She discusses the poverty of feminists (pp. 81 ff.) and touches on the poverty of unmarried women in the nineteenth century (pp. 280–81). As far as her own time is concerned, she expresses a doubt that very many middle-class women will be found who possess independent incomes (p. 168) and asserts that men possess practically all the property in England (p. 33).

than it is usually understood to mean.[13] This may explain her preoccupation with money in *Three Guineas*—the elaborate, and occasionally superfluous, statistics she presented there. She felt impelled to inform her readers, for instance, that the men's scholarship list at Cambridge measures roughly thirty-one inches, the woman's, five inches (pp. 55-56, 277); that the history of Clare College, Cambridge, had cost almost as much to produce (£6000) as the total amount which "Somerville received with pathetic gratitude . . . last year from the Jubilee gift and a private bequest" (p. 273); that Sophia Jex-Blake, in the nineteenth century, "had an allowance of from £30 to £40 annually," Elizabeth Barrett, from £40 to £45 every three months (pp. 280-81); that the salary of an archbishop was £15,000, and of a deaconess, £150 (p. 225). These, and similar bits of information, appear in the notes at the end of *Three Guineas* and are liberally sprinkled throughout the text. One is not altogether certain how to interpret them. In *Orlando* Virginia Woolf had mimicked the solemn biographer with his scholarly apparatus. In *A Room of One's Own* her research into the position of women had been undertaken half archly and had reflected, indirectly, upon masculine pedantry. In *Three Guineas*, on the other hand, she seems for the most part to have intended the documentation to be taken seriously, although echoes of her earlier satirical manner can occasionally be heard. Perhaps she was caught between her respect for science and an innate distrust of fact-finding and statistics that tended to undermine her efforts to marshal the objective evidence in support of her case. She seems, at her worst, to be playing at being a social scientist, and to be achieving not the real thing but a humorless imitation.[14] How is one to react to the idea of Virginia

13   For a discussion of Virginia Woolf's use of the image of the coin in connection with the emancipation of women, see pp. 98-103 below.

14   In *To the Lighthouse* Virginia Woolf humorously described Mrs. Ramsay's attempts to imitate the techniques of the social investigator: "[Mrs. Ramsay] ruminated the . . . problem of rich and poor, and the things she saw with her own eyes, weekly, daily

continued on next page

Woolf, ruler in hand, measuring the scholarship lists for men and women at Cambridge?

Equally interesting for the light it casts upon the way in which Virginia Woolf's mind worked is the fact that, in at least one place, she attributed the poverty of women to excessive childbearing. In *A Room of One's Own* she wrote of visiting her friend Mary Seton at a fictitious women's college, Fernham; of being struck by the extreme meagerness of the comforts that women could afford; and of finding a photograph of Mary's mother upon the mantelpiece, much as Rachel Vinrace had come upon a similar photograph in *The Voyage Out*. Mrs. Seton, like Mrs. Murgatroyd, was intended to be an embodiment of domestic slavery, "a homely body . . . in a plaid shawl . . . encouraging a spaniel to look at the camera, with the amused, yet strained expression of one who is sure that the dog will move directly the bulb is pressed" (p. 35). Why, Virginia Woolf inquired, had not Mrs. Seton gone into business, made a fortune, and left a large legacy to Fernham College, in which case she and Mary might now have been enjoying some of the same creature comforts as the members of the men's colleges? The question was superfluous, considering the fact that Mrs. Seton had borne thirteen children to Mary's father, a minister of the church. "Making a fortune and bearing thirteen children—no human being could stand it" (p. 37). Constant childbearing had kept Mrs. Seton poor, and perhaps, like Susan in *The Waves*, she had felt herself becoming "debased and hide-bound by the bestial and beautiful passion of maternity" (p. 94). Finally, in *Three Guineas*, Virginia Woolf equated "the intensive childbirth of the unpaid wife" with "the intensive money-making of the paid husband in the Victorian age." Both had had

[14] *continued*

> . . . when she visited this widow, or that struggling wife in person with a bag on her arm, and a note-book and pencil with which she wrote down in columns carefully ruled for the purpose wages and spendings, employment and unemployment, in the hope that thus she would cease to be a private woman . . . and become what with her untrained mind she greatly admired, an investigator, elucidating the social problem" (pp. 17–18).

"terrible results," she wrote, ". . . upon the mind and body of the present age" (p. 143). The wife's profession was no less exacting than that of her husband; the only difference was that she received no salary in return for her labors.

Associated in Virginia Woolf's mind with poverty were a group of related grievances: the political helplessness of middle-class women, the difficulties that confronted them in finding work and entering the professions. As far as politics was concerned, such power as women had enjoyed in the past had been in the hands of a few great ladies who had been backed by great fortunes. The old argument that the middle-class woman exerted a hidden influence upon her husband and brother simply did not correspond to the observable facts; the length of time—over a century—which it had taken her to win the franchise proved that the practical effectiveness of her influence was extremely limited. "We can only conclude that influence has to be combined with wealth in order to be effective as a political weapon, and that influence of the kind that can be exerted by the daughters of educated men is very low in power, very slow in action, and very painful in use."[15] As far as the professions were concerned, the position of women was still extremely precarious. The Army and Navy, the Stock Exchange, the Church, the diplomatic corps, all were closed to them. And it had been "decided . . . at a conference of head masters that women were not fit teachers for boys over the age of fourteen" (p. 160). Women had been admitted to the civil service, but, as Virginia Woolf pointed out at length, they had been excluded by a conspiracy of men from the upper, and even the intermediate, ranks of the profession; the same was true in most fields of endeavor.[16] Every advance had been made in face of the determined opposition of men. For the professions, she concluded, "have a certain undeniable effect upon the professors. They make the people who practice them possessive, jealous of any infringement of their rights, and highly combative if anyone dares dispute them" (p. 121).

[15]   *Three Guineas*, p. 27.
[16]   See *ibid.*, pp. 82–95.

Being fully convinced that women are a subject race, Virginia Woolf carried her analysis of society to its logical conclusion. The interests of women, she wrote, have always been identified with those of the men with whom they live, but they are not the same. Her reasoning proceeded along the following lines: from the political and sociological points of view, women form a separate class; the division between the sexes is surely as significant as the differences between working class, middle class, and aristocracy. The fact that women lack political power, for instance, has been obscured by habits of mind which make no clear distinction between the power belonging to a woman and that belonging to her husband or father. The very words people use make it difficult for them to perceive the truth, for the language assumes identities between the sexes which do not, in fact, exist. Obviously, before an injustice can be redressed, she reasoned, it must first be perceived as such; therefore reforms in thought are essential if women are to be emancipated. In order to free ourselves of the old preconceptions, we must create new categories, not referring exclusively to sexual characteristics, by means of which we will be able to distinguish women more precisely from other classes in society. "In a transitional age," she wrote, "when many qualities are changing their value, new words to express new values are much to be desired." It was for this reason that Virginia Woolf referred to certain groups of women as "educated men's daughters" or "outsiders," adopted terms like "unpaid-for education," and expressed doubts whether her countrywomen could rightly be called "English" since they had so little share in the material wealth of England.[17]

Our ideology is still so inveterately anthropocentric [she explained in *Three Guineas*] that it has been necessary to coin this clumsy term—educated man's daughter—to describe the class whose fathers have been educated at public schools and universities. Obviously, if the term "bourgeois" fits her brother,

---

[17]   See *ibid.*, p. 144. Elsewhere she says that the educated man's daughter, after World War I, gained the "right to call herself, if not a full daughter, still a stepdaughter of England" (*ibid.*, p. 23).

it is grossly incorrect to use it of one who differs so profoundly in the two prime characteristics of the bourgeoisie—capital and environment [p. 265].

Another way in which Virginia Woolf emphasized the division between the sexes was by referring to men and women separately, rather than collectively; she spoke of women as "we," of men as "you," till, occasionally, one has the feeling that she is referring to alien races, inhabitants of opposing city-states, rather than to brothers and sisters, husbands and wives living under the same roofs. Here again are her words in *Three Guineas*:

The two classes [men and women] . . . differ enormously. And to prove this, we need not have recourse to the dangerous and uncertain theories of psychologists and biologists; we can appeal to facts. Take the fact of education. Your class has been educated at public schools and universities for five or six hundred years, ours for sixty. Take the fact of property. Your class possesses . . . practically all the capital, all the land, all the valuables, and all the patronage in England. Our class . . . practically none. . . . That such differences make for very considerable differences in mind and body, no psychologist or biologist would deny. It would seem to follow then as an indisputable fact that "we"—meaning by "we" a whole made up of body, brain and spirit . . . must still differ in some essential respects from "you," whose body, brain and spirit have been so differently trained. . . . Though we see the same world, we see it through different eyes [pp. 33-34].

In accordance with her conviction that the sexes are equivalent to dominant and subject races, Virginia Woolf frequently compared women to persecuted minorities; she could not, it would seem, name any downtrodden group, any underdog, without pointing out the parallel with women. Her response to an appeal from the chairman of a society to protect intellectual liberty and culture illustrates her frame of mind. What! she gasped in mock astonishment, a man asking the help of a woman in such a cause? Why, it's as if "the Duke of Devonshire, in his star and garter, stepped down into the kitchen" and asked "the maid who was peeling potatoes with a smudge on her cheek" to help construe a difficult passage in Pindar. Surely the bewildered girl would be justified in exclaiming, "Lawks . . . Master must be mad!"[18] Women as a class, Virginia Woolf implied, are comparable to the humblest of domestic servants. This item in the survey of oppression was echoed and repeated with variations in many other passages. Women, especially when they are feminists, she said, have been subjected to persecutions similar to those of Jews and democrats by the Nazis.[19] Women writers suffer as much from self-consciousness and provincialism as American novelists. They too "are conscious of their own peculiarities as a sex [*sic*]; apt to suspect insolence, quick to avenge grievances, eager to shape an art of their own."[20] Furthermore, women have hitherto had "less intellectual freedom than the sons of Athenian slaves," and therefore "have not had a dog's chance of writing poetry."[21] Women are despised, like the members of the colonial races; they have had as little chance of realizing their genius as the sons of the working classes.[22] They are as easily intimidated as homosexuals.[23] Finally, ironically, Virginia Woolf suggested that women may be likened to the lowliest, and most familiar subject race of all. In *Jacob's Room* the impropriety of permitting women into church wearing whole shopfuls of bright clothes seemed to her equal only to that of letting a dog wander down the aisle, "Looking, lifting a paw, and approaching a pillar with a purpose that makes the blood run cold with horror . . . a dog destroys the service completely. So do these women" (p. 31). The suggestion was taken up again in *Flush*, the biography of Elizabeth Barrett Browning's spaniel, a book full of comparisons between the dog and the poetess, all tending to show that the animal enjoyed considerably more freedom than his mistress. "Hers was the pale

18 *Ibid.*, p. 155.
19 See *ibid.*, pp. 187, 298.
20 "American Fiction," *The Moment*, p. 96.
21 *A Room of One's Own*, p. 188.
22 See *ibid.*, pp. 84, 88.
23 In *Between the Acts* Isabella identifies her own fear of her husband with the homosexual William Dodge's unwillingness to stick up for his beliefs (see p. 50). Later on, they have a moment of recognition in which they see each other as fellow "conspirators" (p. 114).

worn face of an invalid, cut off from air, light, freedom. His was the warm ruddy face of a young animal; instinct with health and energy" (p. 31). Virginia Woolf implied that the lassitude of the woman was, to a large extent, due to the effects of paternal tyranny.

At least as far as material opportunities were concerned, Virginia Woolf saw the position of women in the blackest possible light. The facts were known to all; she consistently interpreted them as proving that the condition of women had always been, and still remained, little better than slavery. She condemned the traditional culture which she had inherited for not having advanced beyond "half-civilized barbarism," for preserving "an eternity of dominion on the one hand and of servility on the other," and concluded that "the degradation of being a slave is only equalled by the degradation of being a master."[24]

2

Virginia Woolf went beyond a mere enumeration of grievances. She attacked the patriarchal order on general, philosophical grounds. The masculine society had confined nature within rigid conventions; the masculine intellect had narrowed the range of experience by imposing its categories too arbitrarily. Order was necessary and desirable, but this extreme emphasis on system amounted to a disease of the spirit. Deposits of habit, combining with self-interest, had slowly encrusted the social structure; the scaffolding intended to support life had become a means of imprisoning it. The tools of analysis, in the hands of scholars and specialists, had turned into manacles. To women who were free of unreal loyalties "to old schools . . . old churches, old ceremonies, old countries," the values of the patriarchal society seemed almost incomprehensible.

[24]   Letter to editor, *New Statesman*, October 16, 1920, p. 46.

Virginia Woolf came to regard most of the venerable institutions of England with suspicion and distaste. A salient
vice of the patriarchal society was its establishment of hierarchies where there was no need of them, where, in fact,
they could only be harmful.[25] Men attempted to measure and
grade everything; the university system, with its honors and
distinctions, graded intellectual merit just as if it were labeling
parcels in a grocer's shop. "But, here, instead of saying 'This
is margarine; this pure butter; this is the finest butter in the
market,' it says, 'This man is a clever man—he is Master of
Arts; this man is a very clever man—he is Doctor of Letters;
this man is a most clever man—he is a Member of the Order
of Merit.'" The effect of this materialism upon the universities themselves was to turn them into "cities of strife, cities
where this is locked up and that is chained down; where
nobody can walk freely or talk freely for fear of transgressing
some chalk mark."[26] Similarly, the church makes it its business to distinguish the gradations of virtue, Virginia Woolf
observed in her essay on Archbishop Thomson. She proceeded ironically to testify to her "simple faith that the outer
order corresponds to the inner—that a vicar is a good man, a
canon a better man, and an archbishop the best man of all."[27]
No doubt the latter is the equivalent, in the moral sphere, of
the "finest butter in the market."

Perhaps the most basic example of this tendency to rank in
hierarchies was the differentiation of society itself into classes.
People were graded socially according to a system comparable to the division of a theater into sections. "To prevent us
from being submerged by chaos, nature and society between
them have arranged a system of classification which is simplicity itself; stalls, boxes, amphitheatre, gallery." Thus she
observed in *Jacob's Room* (p. 67). The manifest pride which
she took not only in belonging to the educated class, but in

[25] Cf. Mary Wollstonecraft's protest against the masculine professions:
"every profession, in which great subordination of rank constitutes
its power, is highly injurious to morality." *A Vindication of the
Rights of Women* (Everyman [London, 1929]), p. 19.
[26] *Three Guineas*, pp. 38, 63.
[27] In *The Common Reader* (1st ser.), p. 281.

being a "lady," did not prevent her from numbering the class system as one of the patriarchical abuses and looking forward to the day when middle-class women would enter, "in the spirit of fellowship into those small, scented rooms where sit the courtesan, the harlot and the lady with the pug-dog." Ultimately, perhaps, her own class might rid itself of "that self-consciousness in the presence of 'sin' which is the legacy of our sexual barbarity," and shake off "the shoddy old fetters of class."[28] Perhaps the best way to sum up her complicated attitude to the class question is to place side by side the comments of two writers who were also her friends. "She felt herself to be not only a woman but a lady," said E. M. Forster. "She was a lady, by birth and upbringing, and it was no use being cowardly about it, and pretending that her mother had turned a mangle, or that [her father] Sir Leslie had been a plasterer's mate. Working-class writers often mentioned their origins, and were respected for doing so. Very well; she would mention hers. And her snobbery—for she was a snob—had more courage in it than arrogance."[29] She was unwilling, and unable, to repudiate the advantages that had come to her by birth; but, as the second comment reminds us, she was deeply critical of the system from which

[28] *A Room of One's Own*, pp. 153, 154. Also see her essay, "The Leaning Tower," in which she commented on the erosion of the class structure and its effects on the writer's task. Here she used a different metaphor for the division of society into classes. "To the nineteenth-century writer human life must have looked like a landscape cut up into separate fields. In each field was gathered a different group of people. Each to some extent had its own traditions; its own manners; its own speech; its own dress; its own occupations . . . a herd grazing within its own hedges." Further on in the essay she conjectured that "the novel of a classless . . . world should be a better novel than the old novel. The novelist will have more interesting people to describe—people who have had a chance to develop their humour, their gifts, their tastes; real people, not people cramped and squashed into featureless masses by hedges." While she recognized that real efforts were now being made to educate the lower classes, she saw England as guilty of a "criminal injustice" in leaving the masses illiterate, or half-educated (*The Moment*, pp. 109, 122, 123).
[29] *Virginia Woolf* (Cambridge, 1942), p. 24.

they sprang. Stephen Spender in a reminiscence of her says that "she had a passionate social curiosity about the 'high' the 'middle' and the 'low' (I am sure these distinctions of class existed sharply in her mind). The British Royal Family was a subject of intense interest to her, partly, I think because as an institution it was a supreme and fascinating example of male pretension which she saw, gold-brocaded, strutting, and stiff in her mind's picture of public life."[30] According to Virginia Woolf the ceremonial dress commonly worn by men on solemn occasions revealed a passion for hierarchies. Ordinarily, their clothes were simple in the extreme, but when they took part in a public function they were robed in almost barbaric splendor. Furthermore, decorations, insignia, uniforms, were not worn merely for aesthetic reasons—if they had been, she would not have found them disturbing—they had the more practical function of advertising "the social, professional, or intellectual standing of the wearer."[31] Similarly, the mumbo-jumbo of rites, ceremonies, initiations, was a kind of splendid institutional garment in which rank was indicated by one's position on the dais or in the procession. And these distinctions, these divisions within society, especially when they were publicly advertised by a uniform, or a medal, or a title in front of one's name, tended to rouse the worst instincts of "competition and jealousy." As a symbolic reflection of certain characteristics of the patriarchy—the desire for possession, for conquest—Virginia Woolf found this mummery not only distasteful, but sinister. In this seemingly trivial custom of wearing buttons, rosettes, stripes, she felt that she could detect the seeds of war. "Obviously the connection . . . is not far to seek," she observed in *Three Guineas*; "your finest clothes are those that you wear as soldiers" (p. 39). She concluded, therefore, with asperity, "that to express worth of any kind, whether intellectual or moral, by wearing pieces of metal, or ribbon, coloured hoods or gowns, is a barbarity which deserves the ridicule which we

---

[30]   "The Life of Literature IV," *Partisan Review*, 16 (February, 1949):
190.
[31]   *Three Guineas*, p. 38.

bestow upon the rites of savages" (pp. 38-39).[32]

Virginia Woolf's aversion to hierarchies led to a prejudice against joining associations of any kind. She refused, for instance, to permit herself to be enrolled in a society for preventing war, in spite of the fact that she sympathized with its aims. Women are different from men, she said, and in order to help the common cause they must be true to themselves. It is not in their true nature to join societies; rules of order and tables of organization are products of the masculine mind. If women were to have a society at all, it should be one with "no office, no committee, no secretary; it would call no meetings; it would hold no conferences. If name it must have, it could be called the Outsiders' Society."[33] For, as she explained to the gentleman who had asked her support, the very sound of the word "society" suggests images of oppression to a woman. "Inevitably we look upon societies as conspiracies that . . . inflate . . . a monstrous male, loud of voice, hard of fist, childishly intent upon scoring the floor of the earth with chalk marks, within whose mystic boundaries human beings are penned, rigidly, separately, artificially; where . . . decorated like a savage with feathers he goes through mystic rites and enjoys the dubious pleasures of

---

[32] Virginia Woolf emphasized her point about clothes in *Three Guineas* by interspersing the text with photographs of masculine functionaries in ceremonial garb—mute testimonials to the wickedness of pomp, and power. The functionaries are identified in the list of illustrations as A General, Heralds, A University Procession, A Judge, An Archbishop. Traces of this attitude may be found in the novels—*Mrs. Dalloway*, for instance, where it seems more than a coincidence that Lady Bradshaw's portrait, hanging on her husband's office wall, shows the enslaved woman in Court dress, invested with the livery, so to speak, of the oppressors (see p. 108). Hugh Whitbread, another notable example of a one-sided male in *Mrs. Dalloway*, is a Court servant, and performs his duties in ceremonial uniform. In *To the Lighthouse*, when Mrs. Ramsay wins over Charles Tansley by "insinuating . . . the greatness of man's intellect . . . the subjection of all wives . . . to their husband's labours," he wishes that she could "see him, gowned and hooded, walking in a procession" (p. 20).

[33] *Three Guineas*, p. 193.

power and dominion."[34] Societies, the practice of grading
and ranking, the splendor of ceremonial dress, the barbaric
urge to aggression—all were related; all formed part of the
patriarchal institutions, the mysteries of the male sex. It made
little difference whether the ranking was accomplished by
sewing on colored bits of ribbon or by the device of drawing
chalk marks on the floor. Everywhere one walked, she ex-
claimed, one seemed to encounter the chalk marks, rigid
divisions, which, though they could hardly be said to have
substance at all, were often more confining than bars of
steel.[35] The most striking examples of such intangible restraints could, perhaps, be drawn from the preceding century.
Take, for instance, the daily life of a girl in an average Victorian home: "When she thought of their day it seemed to
her that it was cut into four pieces by their meals. These
divisions were absolutely rigid, the contents of the day having
to accommodate themselves within the four rigid bars. Looking back at her life, that was what she saw."[36] The contrast
between the rigidity of the divisions and the insipidness of
the contents was especially disturbing. Victorian society, of
course, had been notable for the proliferation of chalk marks.

There was a rule for everything [Virginia Woolf mused in
"The Mark on the Wall"]. The rule for tablecloths at that
particular period was that they should be made of tapestry with
little yellow compartments marked upon them. . . . Tablecloths

---

[34] *Ibid.*, p. 191. The image of "mystic boundaries" within which
human beings are penned is obviously related to that of the
hedges by means of which, Virginia Woolf says, society is divided
into classes. See note 28, above. In her essay "Memories of a
Working Women's Guild" she stated her objection to societies in
a more general form: "When people get together communally
. . . they always show the least desirable of their characteristics—
their lust for conquest and their desire for possessions" (*The
Captain's Death Bed*, p. 214).

[35] Virginia Woolf first introduced the image of the chalk marks in
The Voyage Out. Terence Hewet uses it in speaking of his friend,
Hirst, a typical exponent of the masculine intellect. " 'I'm not like
Hirst,' said Hewet . . .'I don't see circles of chalk between people's
feet. I sometimes wish I did' " (p. 218).

[36] The girl is Rachel Vinrace in *The Voyage Out,* p. 214.

of a different kind were not real tablecloths. . . . What now takes the place of those things I wonder, those real standard things? Men perhaps, should you be a woman; the masculine point of view which governs our lives, which sets the standard, which established Whitaker's Table of Precedency.[37]

And in Whitaker's Table of Precedency we have an important manifestation of the chalk marks, for Whitaker informs us that "the Archbishop of Canterbury is followed by the Lord High Chancellor; the Lord High Chancellor . . . by the Archbishop of York." It is the apotheosis of hierarchy. "Everybody follows somebody, such is the philosophy of Whitaker; and the great thing is to know who follows whom."[38] Whitaker was a recurring symbol, in Virginia Woolf's feminist writings, of the masculine propensity for ranking and measuring.[39] The same hatred of arbitrary chalk marks may be inferred from many episodes in her novels, and these show how widely she applied her ideas. In *The Waves*, for instance, young Susan hates school because her nature rebels against the rigidity of schedules, because schoolmistresses "have made all the days of June . . . shiny and orderly." Even piano lessons, which involve the playing of scales, have, for the little girl, something unwholesome and arbitrary about them (pp. 29, 32). Is it perhaps because a scale is something measured? Similarly in *Night and Day*, William Rodney writes lines of poetry that display a remarkable skill in metrics but have a tendency to put the listener to sleep. His mastery of the techniques of prosody—a skill which, Katharine reflects, is "almost exclusively masculine"—is contrasted with his apparent lack of real poetic talent (p. 140). Nor did Virginia Woolf spare the critic, with his attempts to rank and measure works of literature. "Delightful as the pastime of measuring may be, it is the most futile of all occupations," she advised young writers in *A Room of One's Own*.

[37] In *A Haunted House*, p. 44.
[38] *Ibid.*, p. 46.
[39] For other references to Whitaker, see *Three Guineas*, pp. 83–95, 158; *A Room of One's Own*, p. 184. Is Virginia Woolf's choice of a name for the evil doctor in *Mrs. Dalloway* possibly to be connected with *Bradshaw's Monthly Railway Guide*?

And "to sacrifice a hair of the head of your vision . . . in deference to some Headmaster . . . or to some professor with a measuring-rod up his sleeve, is the most abject treachery" (p. 185).

In the area of intellectual life, the influence of the chalk marks was to inhibit or pervert natural growth. The average professional man suffered, both intellectually and morally, from the masculine disease of specialization. Visiting one of the universities, Virginia Woolf found the scholars "creased and crushed into shapes so singular that one was reminded of those giant crabs and crayfish who heave with difficulty across the sand of an aquarium."[40] In her early satirical story, "A Society," she described the ruinous education to which the professional man was subjected:

> What could be more charming than a boy before he has begun to cultivate his intellect? He is beautiful to look at; he gives himself no airs; he understands the meaning of art and literature instinctively. . . . Then they teach him to cultivate his intellect. He becomes a barrister, a civil servant, a general, an author, a professor. Every day he goes to an office. Every year he produces a book. . . . Soon he cannot come into a room without making us all feel uncomfortable; he condescends to every woman he meets and dares not tell the truth even to his own wife.[41]

There is perhaps an element of "sour grapes" in this condemnation. For, as we have seen, Virginia Woolf was indignant at the exclusion of women from the universities and fiercely coveted the educational advantages enjoyed by men. Her position can be reduced to the contradictory formula that, if it is impossible to abolish the evils of the educational establishment, women at least should be permitted to suffer their effects on a basis of full equality with men. Ideally, as we shall see, she favored an educational system that would do away with the evils of competition and specialization while preserving the advantages of academic training. She acknowledged, however, that the ideal was not very likely to be achieved in this world.

[40] *A Room of One's Own*, p. 13.
[41] In *Monday or Tuesday*, pp. 33–34.

Her attitude toward professional life shows a similar pattern. She demanded equal opportunities for women in the professions while deploring the conditions under which they would have to work. In *Three Guineas* she gathered evidence of the effects the professions have upon those who practice them. She found a politician saying that since 1914 he had "never seen the pageant of the blossom from the first damson to the last apple—never once. . . ." A bishop, referring to the pressures of his work, protested that it was "an awful mind-and-soul-destroying life" (pp. 128, 129). A doctor, who was making more than £13,000 a year, called his existence slavery. That is why bishops and doctors can heal neither soul nor body. Professional life, she contended, destroys the man and creates a monster. "If people are highly successful in their professions they lose their senses. Sight goes. They have no time to look at pictures. Sound goes. They have no time to listen to music. Speech goes. They have no time for conversation. They lose their sense of proportion. . . . Humanity goes. . . . Health goes. . . . What then remains of a human being who has lost sight, and sound, and sense of proportion? Only a cripple in a cave" (pp. 131–32). Professional life thus frequently involved a paradox to which Virginia Woolf alluded in her essay on "Archbishop Thomson." The Archbishop, she informed her readers, had "turned aside from poetry and philosophy and law, and specialized in virtue." But, she asked at the conclusion of the essay, "is it easy, is it possible, for a good man to be an Archbishop?"[42] Elsewhere, she questioned whether renowned scholars, who spend their time "brawling about Greek and Latin texts, and calling each other names for all the world like bookies on a racecourse" can be relied upon to convey the truth of the classics?[43] It would seem that the very process of becoming an archbishop, a scholar, of turning aside from all other interests and specializing in virtue, or ancient languages, would prevent one from being a good man, or a wise one.

The chalk marks were antilife forces, so to speak; they

---

[42]   *The Common Reader* (1st ser.), pp. 281, 286.
[43]   "Dr. Bentley" in "Outlines," *ibid.*, p. 270.

inhibited and confined. But, as I have already suggested, Virginia Woolf believed that the patriarchal order also fostered impulses that destroy life directly: the lust for possession, for war. The patriarchs and professors have acquired money and power, she pointed out, "only at the cost of harbouring in their breasts . . . a vulture, for ever tearing the liver out and plucking at the lungs . . . which drives them to desire other people's fields and goods perpetually . . . to offer up their own lives and their children's lives."[44] She stated the idea that war is exclusively masculine most baldly in *Three Guineas*: "to fight has always been the man's habit, not the woman's. . . . Scarcely a human being in the course of history has fallen to a woman's rifle; the vast majority of birds and beasts have been killed by you, not by us" (pp. 13-14).

Perhaps with this last assertion we should stop for a moment to review our impressions and to draw a sketch of the evil patriarch as Virginia Woolf saw him. By means of the composite image we catch a glimpse of a twisted monster; one hand holds a yardstick, the other points a gun. It is a startling apparition, far uglier than any actual creature that walks in the pages of her books; nevertheless, some such vision must at times have troubled her mind. It is as if she had met a horror once, at dead of night, and has left traces of the encounter scattered about in her writings. She was filled with a desire to destroy his power, to break out of the shell of system and convention which he had created, but where was one to begin? For he permeated everything; his shadow was even upon the societies that were dedicated to opposing him.

Several writers have noted Virginia Woolf's ambivalent attitude toward the feminist societies, as distinct from the feminist cause. Clive Bell, in a reminiscence of his sister-in-law, asserts flatly that "in political feminism—the Suffrage Movement—she was not much interested." Bell goes on to comment: "I do remember that once or twice she and I went to some obscure office where we licked up envelopes for the

44 *A Room of One's Own*, pp. 65-66.

Adult Suffrage League. But . . . it was not in political action
that her feminism expressed itself: indeed she made merciless
fun of the flag-wagging fanaticism of her old friend Ethel
Smythe."[45] James Hafley observes with interest that "*Night
and Day* is anything but friendly to reform societies in general
and feminism in particular."[46] And Joan Bennett suggests
that, "in her novels, women of action, even those who embrace the Feminist Cause, are perceived as a little comic. . . .
There is some oscillation in *Night and Day*," she adds,
"between ridicule and admiration for Mrs. Seal, the active
feminist. . . . Mary Datchet certainly is both admirable and
lovable; but then her activities are, in the main, palliatives
for her private sorrows."[47]

Virginia Woolf had doubts about the suffrage societies
because she felt that they borrowed their weapons from the
enemy; they too were hierarchical organizations, with committees and rules, and to that extent, unfeminine. She feared
contact with the infectious evils she was combatting. This
attitude is reflected in the aristocratic aloofness of Katharine
Hilbery in *Night and Day*. Katharine, visiting her friend Mary
Datchet at the office of a suffrage society where she works, is
set upon and catechized by Mrs. Seal, a woolly-headed
feminist. When Katharine announces that she is in favor of
votes for women, Mrs. Seal demands to know why she is not
a member of their society. Katharine remains silent. A little
later the same question is put to her by a neutral observer, and
she replies, "O dear no—that wouldn't do at all" (p. 94). It is
clear that, on this point, Virginia Woolf shared Katharine's
reticence, and, perhaps, her embarrassment. Her treatment

---

[45] "Virginia Woolf," *Old Friends*, p. 101.
[46] *The Glass Roof: Virginia Woolf as Novelist* (Berkeley, 1954), p. 33.
"Mary Datchet," Hafley writes, "is presented as a sincere and
sympathetic character (and clumsily disposed of for that reason). . . .
Katharine pictures the feminist workers 'murmuring their
incantations and concocting their drugs, and flinging their frail
spiders' webs over the torrents of life which rushed down the
streets outside.' Katharine is in favor of the goals of feminism but
not of these means for obtaining them" (pp. 33-34).
[47] *Virginia Woolf: Her Art as a Novelist* (Cambridge, 1945), p. 76.

The Sins of the Fathers

of the suffrage society was comic, as the names of Mary Datchet's co-workers, Mr. Clacton and Mrs. Seal, suggest. Mr. Clacton, a timid little man with "a frugal look, as if nature had not dealt generously with him in any way, which, naturally, prevented him from dealing generously with other people," is guilty of speaking with a Cockney accent and of cultivating an interest in literature (p. 80). Mrs. Seal, who was "always in a hurry, and always in some disorder . . . wore two crucifixes, which got themselves entangled in a heavy gold chain upon her breast, and seemed . . . expressive of her mental ambiguity" (p. 81). Further glimpses of these two reformers in action do little to reassure the reader as to the future of the Cause.

But Virginia Woolf's observations on the suffrage society have their serious side. Mary Datchet, the idealistic secretary of the society, stands for what is best in the organized movement for reform. Mary remains a complex human being; she has never specialized in "virtue" to such an extent as to transform herself into the mere enthusiast of a cause. Unlike Mr. Clacton and Mrs. Seal, she recognizes that the chief good in life is to be sought in a realm altogether beyond the world of reforming societies and politics. Mary is not fully committed to a career of reform, she still has a hope of finding fulfillment in private life, but this hope is tied up with her love for Ralph Denham. When she learns that Ralph loves Katharine, the prospect closes before her, and she feels that she has no choice but to throw in her lot with Mr. Clacton and Mrs. Seal, who, at any rate, are working for a better world. She knows the full implications of the commitment.

She had entered in the army, and was a volunteer no longer. She had renounced something and was now—how could she express it?—not quite "in the running" for life. She had always known that Mr. Clacton and Mrs. Seal were not in the running, and across the gulf that separated them she had seen them in the guise of shadow people, flitting in and out of the ranks of the living—eccentrics, undeveloped human beings, from whose substance some essential part had been cut away. All this had never struck her so clearly as it did this afternoon, when she felt that her lot was cast with them for ever [p. 265].

In the aridity of these "shadow people," in the sense that "some essential part had been cut away," we are shown the tribute that the patriarchal order exacts from those who oppose it. Antagonism, strangely enough, seems to make the reformer resemble, in some ways, those against whom he is fighting. Mr. Clacton and Mrs. Seal have this in common with the patriarchs: they have sacrificed a part of their humanity. And Mary Datchet, in deciding to turn aside and specialize in women's rights, will perhaps lose something, like the Archbishop, and suffer to some extent the fate of a "cripple in a cave."

At the furthest extreme in the process of alienation stands Miss Kilman, who teaches modern history to Mrs. Dalloway's daughter, Elizabeth. She is, in a sense, the female counterpart of Sir William Bradshaw; her existence overshadows the life of Clarissa as Sir William's does that of Septimus.[48] Miss Kilman is an emancipated woman who supports herself; her way of life, her staunch support of the causes she believes in, are possible because women have finally won the right to earn a living. But her emancipation is altogether illusory; in fact, the bitterness of her struggles in a hostile environment has perverted her nature. She is possessed by the enemy. The evils of the patriarchal society are reflected in her one-sidedness as they are in that of Sir William. The identification of Miss Kilman with the patriarchs is apparent early in the book. "It was not her one hated," Clarissa notes, "but the idea of her, which undoubtedly had gathered in to itself a great deal that was not

---

[48]   Cf. D. S. Savage's comment: "It would seem that just as Clarissa
        Dalloway and Septimus Warren Smith are linked through their
        passive openness to life in a sort of unconscious psychic sympathy,
        so the decisive attitudes of Miss Kilman and Sir William Bradshaw
        together converge upon that threatening imperative toward
        conversion, the imposition of a definite view of life upon the
        fluid, the indefinite, which is felt as inexpressibly menacing to
        everything that Clarissa Dalloway herself values and represents."
        "The Mind of Virginia Woolf," *South Atlantic Quarterly Review*
        (October, 1947), p. 564. This article is an attack upon Virginia
        Woolf for her "inability to make any decisive movement of
        belief" (p. 560).

Miss Kilman; had become one of those spectres with which one battles in the night; one of those spectres who stand astride us and suck up half our life-blood, dominators and tyrants" (pp. 14-15). Miss Kilman, too, has been reduced to "a cripple in a cave." "Sometimes lately it had seemed to her that, except for Elizabeth, her food was all that she lived for; her comforts; her dinner, her tea; her hot-water bottle at night" (p. 142). The story of her life is almost a parable. She had been teaching at a school; the war had come; she had been unable to sympathize with the prevalent hatred of Germans—too principled to "pretend that the Germans were all villains—when she had German friends, when the only happy days of her life had been spent in Germany!" (P. 136.) She had had to leave the school. So the patriarchy had robbed her of her livelihood. Then, having reduced her to poverty, it had taken her soul. "Bitter and burning [she] had turned into a church" and been converted by the Rev. Edward Whittaker, a namesake of the Almanac-maker (p. 137). Mr. Whittaker had assured her that "she was there for a purpose," and that "knowledge comes through suffering" (pp. 142, 143). But her newly found religion had not softened her bitterness; it had merely provided a channel for her fanaticism. In her piety she had found a new pretext for making people uncomfortable, for hating them. Even Elizabeth, who is under her influence, perceives that there is some contradiction in her Christian doctrine. "If it was being on committees and giving up hours and hours every day . . . that helped the poor, her father did that, goodness knows—if that was what Miss Kilman meant about being a Christian," Elizabeth ponders (p. 150). The similarity between Miss Kilman's "Christianity" and the reforming program of the practical politician is significant. It is another way of suggesting that Miss Kilman, weak, ugly, friendless, has become one of the "shadow people" and now inhabits a remote corner of the cave.

> The religious ecstasy made people callous (so did causes) . . . [Clarissa concluded] for Miss Kilman would do anything for the Russians, starved herself for the Austrians, but in private inflicted positive torture, so insensitive was she, dressed in a green mackintosh coat. Year in year out she wore that coat;

she perspired; she was never in the room five minutes without making you feel her superiority, your inferiority; how poor she was; how rich you were [p. 14].

As a pun, Miss Kilman's name alludes not so much to hatred of the masculine sex, as to hatred of mankind. She embodies the familiar dangers of fanatical devotion to a cause: alienation from life, a tendency to worship abstractions and to hate people as individuals.[49] The feminist movement, as Virginia Woolf saw it, was by no means exempt from these dangers.

But, although she had doubts about the suffrage societies, and deprecated the violence of the militants ("Force is always wrong," she made Eleanor comment in *The Years*, while, about the same time, she was advocating pacifism in *Three Guineas*)—although the societies left much to be desired, Virginia Woolf had no doubts that the feminist movement represented what was best in the political life of England. She was quick to resent the use of the word "feminist" as a derogatory label. In order to prevent this abuse she advocated the abolition of the word altogether, for was there really such a thing, she asked, as a feminist? Why should not those who had fought against the oppression of women simply be classed with other fighters against tyranny?

[49] Miss Kilman belongs to a class of women—poor, half educated, struggling to earn a living by teaching—for whom Virginia Woolf generally had a good deal of sympathy. (Cf. Miss Craddock, who teaches Kitty in *The Years*, pp. 63–66.) It is interesting, therefore, that in this case even Miss Kilman's qualifications as a victim of the patriarchy fail to win her Virginia Woolf's sympathies. Miss Kilman's antagonist, Clarissa Dalloway, belongs to a fashionable clique with which Virginia Woolf never had much in common, but she obviously found it easier to forgive Clarissa's snobbishness than Kilman's lower-class vulgarity. Whatever the distance that separated the daughter of Leslie Stephen from the members of the fashionable world—and she was at times painfully aware of being a social misfit—it was slight compared to the gulf between her and those who remained on the other side of the class barrier. Her feelings of dislike for the woman of fashion, moreover, were alloyed with envy. She partly shared Helen Ambrose's conviction in *The Voyage Out* that all men, even intellectual men, "prefer women to be fashionable" (p. 46).

"What were they working for in the nineteenth century—
those queer dead women in their poke bonnets and shawls?
. . . They were fighting the same enemy that you are fighting
and for the same reasons. They were fighting the tyranny of
the patriarchal state as you are fighting the tyranny of the
Fascist state."[50] Isn't it time, she suggested, that they were
recognized as "the advance guard of your own movement?"
In any case, now that the "only right, the right to earn a
living," had been won, the word "feminist" could have no
further meaning. Inscribing the word on a sheet of foolscap
and proceeding with a lighted match to cremate the corpse,
she proclaimed, with a bitterness worth noting, that anyone
who used the word in the future was a "ring-the-bell-and-
run-away man, a mischief maker, a groper among old bones,
the proof of whose defilement is written in a smudge of dirty
water upon his face."[51] The petulance of the charge, the
extravagance with which she coined a new expression (meaning "those who make use of words with the desire to hurt
but at the same time to escape detection") indicate how
deeply she still felt the derision to which she had been subjected on account of her views.

There was a note of bitterness too in her reluctance to enter
fully into any movement for reform. "Improving the world
she would not consider," E. M. Forster recalled, "on the
ground that the world is man-made, and that she, a woman,
had no responsibility for the mess."[52] Experience and history
had taught her, she explained in *Three Guineas*, that it was
pointless for women to interfere directly, actively. "We can
only help you to defend culture and intellectual liberty by
defending our own culture and our own intellectual liberty"
(p. 161). Women, she felt, must abstain, must protect themselves from the corruption around them, and cultivate their
gardens, at least until they were cleansed of the sense of
grievance which had poisoned their relations with men. She
looked forward to a time when they would achieve the

---

50   *Three Guineas*, pp. 185–86.
51   *Ibid.*, p. 185; also see note 11, p. 311.
52   *Virginia Woolf: The Rede Lecture* (Cambridge, 1942), p. 8.

freedom which she had attributed to her imaginary novelist, Mary Carmichael, in *A Room of One's Own*: "Men were no longer to her 'the opposing faction'; she need not waste her time railing against them. . . . Fear and hatred were almost gone, or traces of them showed only in a slight exaggeration of the joy of freedom" (pp. 160-61). The foundation upon which this freedom would be based was economic independence. If a woman were to cultivate her garden, she must have money and a room of her own. That is why Virginia Woolf considered the right to earn a living more important than the right to vote.[53] And that is why there are so many seemingly gratuitous references to money in her books.[54] She regularly used the coin as a symbol of certain essential freedoms.

Coin symbolism appears in both Virginia Woolf's feminist writings and her novels. In the feminist writings coins are related primarily to economic independence; in the novels they tend to be related more to inner than to outer freedom, to the core of the individual and the possession of one's soul in peace. In some cases the coin is a simple metaphor; in others, it is used to suggest a complex visionary experience.

Jacob's Room is the earliest of the novels to make deliberate use of coin symbolism. The model, Fanny Elmer, who is in love with Jacob, reflects on the beauty of young men and the freedom of their lives. "And isn't it pleasant, Fanny went on thinking, how young men bring out lots of silver coins from their trouser pockets, and look at them, instead of having

[53] Virginia Woolf states this view in *A Room of One's Own* when the narrator receives word of a legacy left her by her aunt. "The news of my legacy reached me one night about the same time that the act was passed that gave votes to women. . . . Of the two—the vote and the money—the money, I own, seemed infinitely the more important" (p. 63). In considering the requirements of women writers Virginia Woolf did not distinguish between earned and unearned income. She repeatedly stressed, however, that independence must be paid for with cash. Her own income was derived in part from a small inheritance which she supplemented by her earnings as a writer.

[54] See the examples from *Three Guineas*, given above, pp. 76-77.

just so many in a purse?" (P. 117.) The fleeting image reflects the theme of the book. Jacob lives fully and freely, making use of all his faculties, before he is killed in a senseless war. Against the background of his exemplary life Virginia Woolf sets the relatively circumscribed lives of the women with whom he comes in contact. Young men keep their coins loose in their pockets, ready to hand; women hoard a few in a purse. Jacob is able to enjoy all the advantages of freedom and superior culture because he has not yet been spoiled by specialization. On the other hand, Jacob's professor at Cambridge, old Huxtable, keeps his money in a leather purse and grudges "even the smallest silver coin, secretive and suspicious as an old peasant woman" (p. 38).

The more elaborate imagery of coins in *Mrs. Dalloway* has been discussed by John Hawley Roberts. He finds this imagery to be one of the elements which connects the two main characters of the novel, in spite of the fact that they never meet.

> Helping to unite Clarissa and Septimus is the image that likens life to a coin. . . . Clarissa is thinking of the delight she takes in all the objects around her. . . . And suddenly come the words, "She remembered once throwing a shilling into the Serpentine." Immediately, associated with this memory and with her love of life, comes the opposed emotion which accepts death as a consolation. . . . A highly complicated set of feelings and thoughts is established: life, death, the shilling thrown into the Serpentine, her sense of being merged with unknown persons, and—finally—the words "Fear no more the heat of the sun". . . . When the news of Septimus' death reaches Clarissa at her party . . . and she hears that he threw himself from a window, she immediately recalls "that she had once thrown a shilling into the Serpentine, never anything more. But he had flung it away."[55]

Here the image is in reverse, so to speak; the negative act, the throwing away of the coin, has been made to suggest, if not freedom of spirit, at least the pursuit of freedom.

[55] " 'Vision and Design' in Virginia Woolf," *PMLA*, 61 (September, 1946): 838.

In contrast to the complex development of the theme in *Mrs. Dalloway*, Virginia Woolf's use of the coin image in *Three Guineas* is relatively simple. She is stressing the importance of the act which permitted women to enter the professions:

> The door of the private house was thrown open. In every purse there was, or might be, one bright new sixpence in whose light every thought, every sight, every action looked different. . . . The moon even, scarred as it is in fact with forgotten craters, seemed to her a white sixpence, a chaste sixpence, an altar upon which she vowed never to side with the servile, the signers-on, since it was hers to do what she liked with—the sacred sixpence that she had earned with her own hands herself. . . .
>
> She need no longer use her charm to procure money from her father or brother. Since it is beyond the power of her family to punish her financially she can express her own opinions [pp. 30, 32].

As a symbol of economic freedom, the sixpence, for Virginia Woolf, is a fundamental fact of life. Her commitment to female emancipation is revealed simply and starkly in her invocation, where she links the coin with the very Goddess of Feminity.[56]

In *The Years* the coin becomes a central symbol; never losing its solidity, its character as a hard metal disc, it is nevertheless endowed with all the suggestiveness of Mrs. Dalloway's shilling. Like the image of the couple coming home at dawn in a taxi, it gives us inklings of a vision that has haunted Eleanor, a vision that she is unable to express in words. All throughout the final party, Eleanor, who wishes to pay her share for the cab which brought them there, but cannot get her niece Peggy to accept the money, holds coins in her clenched fist. These coins are related in the first place, as in *Three Guineas*, to the emancipation of women.

Many years earlier, Eleanor had been present at the meeting of a feminist society in the very same room where the party is now being given. She had sat there, while the members

56   The same image of the moon as a coin appears at the beginning of *The Years*, p. 4.

bickered, and had drawn a black dot with spokes radiating from it with her pencil on the blotting paper. "If we could only get at something, something deeper, deeper, she thought, prodding her pencil on the blotting-paper. Suddenly she saw the only point that was of any importance. . . . But just as she cleared her throat, Mr. Pickford swept his papers together and rose" (pp. 177–78). And now, sitting at the chaotic party, holding coins in her fist, she searches for meaning in her past. "Millions of things came back to her. Atoms danced apart and massed themselves. But how did they compose what people called a life? She clenched her hands and felt the hard little coins she was holding. Perhaps there's 'I' at the middle of it, she thought; a knot; a centre; and again she saw herself . . . drawing on the blotting-paper, digging little holes from which spokes radiated" (pp. 366–67).[57] Here we catch hold, for a moment, of a strand among the many strands of her experience. The little hole with the spokes radiating from it, the coins in her hands, the suffrage meeting, and the thing that she had seen, the only point that was of any importance —taken together, they begin to form a pattern. Tying in with them is a moment of happiness which overtakes Eleanor a little later on in the party. In spite of the festivities around her, she has been dozing on and off, being carried back into the past, and this experience comes during her sleep. "She felt extraordinarily happy. Most sleep left some dream in one's mind. . . . But this sleep, this momentary trance, in which the candles had lolled and lengthened themselves, had left her with nothing but a feeling; a feeling, not a dream" (p. 381). Waking, Eleanor finds that the others are laughing at her, and in order to shield her new feeling of happiness she suddenly becomes very practical, starts talking about money, and questioning her nephew about his income. He has saved four or five thousand, she learns. " 'Well, that's enough,' she insisted. 'Five per cent; six per cent—' She tried to do the sum in her head. . . . 'Four or five thousand—how much would

[57] Eleanor's memory of drawing on the blotting paper refers not so much to the suffrage meeting as to another time when she sat at her table, making little holes with spokes, but the three episodes are all clearly connected. For this third episode, see p. 102 below.

that be?.... Enough to live on, wouldn't it?' " (P. 382). Then, in a later scene, the connection between the coins in Eleanor's hands and her feeling of happiness is expressly stated; the significance of her happiness begins to appear. She has been dozing again, and slowly comes to herself. "But where was she? In what room? In which of innumerable rooms?... She shut her hands on the coins she was holding, and again she was suffused with a feeling of happiness. Was it because this had survived—this keen sensation (she was waking up) and the other thing, the solid object—she saw an ink-corroded walrus—had vanished?" (P. 426.) Eleanor's memory of the walrus, which her brother Martin gave their mother for her birthday, is yet another link with the Victorian past; it recalls a scene early in the book when Eleanor, still young, sat doing accounts at her writing table. The walrus, worn and frayed even at that time, had already survived the death of Eleanor's mother by several years.

It's awfully queer, she thought, touching the ink-corroded patch of bristle on the back of Martin's walrus with the point of her pen, that *that* should have gone on all these years. That solid object might survive them all. If she threw it away it would still exist somewhere or other. . . . She drew on her blotting paper; a dot with strokes raying out round it. . . . She dipped her pen in the ink.
"Three times eight," she murmured, "is twenty-four" [p. 91].

The party at the end of the novel, as we have seen, shows that it is the "solid object," the walrus, that passes away; that something within the individual endures. Eleanor's discovery of this truth is the source of her happiness, her revelation. And this hard, imperishable substance, whatever it may be, is related to the hard little coins in her hands, to the core of the self, to the drawing of a dot from which spokes radiate, and to the point which Eleanor wished to make at the suffrage meeting. Furthermore, this reality of Eleanor's is both a spiritual principle and a part of the tangible life around her; it is present even in the bickering of the suffrage meeting. The symbol of liberation, the coin, is as material an object as the ink-corroded walrus. This too is part of Eleanor's revelation.

There must be another life, she thought. . . . Not in dreams;
but here and now, in this room, with living people.[58] She felt
as if she were standing on the edge of a precipice with her hair
blown back; she was about to grasp something that just evaded
her. There must be another life, here and now, she repeated.
This is too short, too broken. We know nothing, even about
ourselves. We're only just beginning, she thought, to understand,
here and there. She hollowed her hands in her lap. . . . She held
her hands hollowed; she felt that she wanted to enclose the
present moment; to make it stay; to fill it fuller and fuller, with
the past, the present and the future, until it shone, whole, bright,
deep with understanding [pp. 427-28].[59]

Even when Virginia Woolf's coin symbolism is related to
complex states of mind, as it is in *The Years*, it always retains
its social implications. She never loses sight of the prosaic
object and the economics of daily life. In *The Years* she succeeded in joining social commentary and visionary experience. This achievement stands as a model of the unified vision
which was her ideal.

[58]   Virginia Woolf for a while considered using the phrase "here and
now" as the title of the novel. See *A Writer's Diary*, p. 208.
[59]   A plan for the conclusion of *The Years* that Virginia Woolf jotted
down in her diary while she was at work on the novel—and later
discarded—suggests the importance of the coin in her scheme of
symbolism. "It's to end with Elvira [Eleanor] going out of the
house and saying, 'What did I make this knot in my handkerchief
for? and all the coppers rolling about—' " See *A Writer's Diary*,
August 17, 1934, p. 214. Another instance of coin imagery should
be kept in mind. "There is a spot the size of a shilling at the back
of the head which one can never see for oneself. It is one of the
good offices that sex can discharge for sex—to describe that spot
the size of a shilling at the back of the head" (*A Room of One's
Own*, p. 157).

··❦[4]❧··

The Androgynous Mind

The highest aim of the feminist movement, as Virginia Woolf saw it, was to prepare the way for profound adjustments in the inner lives of the sexes. A marriage had to be consummated, she said, within the mind itself of each individual, a union between the masculine and feminine principles. Social changes were a necessary first step, but they affected only the surface of things. Drawing upon Sophocles' *Antigone*, which for Virgina Woolf was a primer of resistance to masculine tyranny, she discovered the "distinction between laws and the Law." "According to Antigone there are two kinds of law," she pointed out in *Three Guineas*, "the written and the unwritten.... The many and varied activities of the educated man's daughter in the nineteenth century were... endeavours of an experimental kind to discover what are the unwritten laws; that is the private laws that should regulate certain instincts, passions, mental and physical desires" (pp. 323–24). Even when Virginia Woolf was determined, as in *Three Guineas*, to play the role of practical feminist, the policies she advocated had as much to do with the spiritual condition of women as with their worldly success. Her interpretation of the unwritten laws of the mind is an essential part of her feminist doctrine.

Virginia Woolf held that the minds of women differ radically from the minds of men. But the true nature of the difference was just beginning to become apparent; the coins which women were earning enabled them, for the first time, to live their own lives. Since they had been dependent on men for hundreds of years, their manners, their ideas, their very souls, had been modified by the constant pressure of masculine standards. Now they might begin to discover values and life rhythms of their own, without submitting to the criticism of any task-master. For the first time they had an opportunity to be themselves. Virginia Woolf pictured them as strange organisms that had been "under the shadow of the rock these million years" and were now timidly crawling into the light.[1]

External barriers had fallen, but the real struggle for freedom was just beginning. The last stronghold of patriarchal tyranny was in the minds of women themselves, in their adherence to alien modes of thought, in their attempts to be exactly like men, or to differ from them in everything. Self-conscious emulation, self-conscious defiance, both deformed the mind and diverted women from the goal, which was to be themselves. Political feminism could not bring about this freeing of the mind, Virginia Woolf believed, because like all political movements it created divisions in society rather than healing them. But feminists, working as individuals, had been among the first to discover the nature of "the unwritten laws." Virginia Woolf's aim, both as feminist and as artist, was to contribute to this exploration of feminine values. Thus, as Joan Bennett observes, she brought to the feminist cause "something much more interesting and profound than an advocacy of equal rights." It was her real contribution to

[1]   *A Room of One's Own*, p. 147.

unveil "the essential quality of female experience where it differs from the male."[2]

In spite of the profound differences between the sexes, Virginia Woolf held that "it is fatal for any one who writes to think of their sex. It is fatal to be a man or woman pure and simple; one must be woman-manly or man-womanly. It is fatal for a woman to lay the least stress on any grievance . . . in any way to speak consciously as a woman."[3] Women would never free their minds by imitating masculine exclusiveness. They must recognize that both sexes are present in the mind; they must conduct their lives so as to give each element expression, and to join both into a harmonious whole. Then their femininity would cease being a puzzle and a burden to them; they would become truly unconscious of their sex. This ideal appealed to Virginia Woolf precisely because she was so far from attaining it. She could not help brooding about her grievances, although she repeatedly warned others against doing so. Even during middle age, when she had become a famous novelist, any hint of condescension in a man made her suffer agonies.[4] She was vulnerable because, almost in spite of herself, she felt profound

---

[2]   *Virginia Woolf: Her Art as a Novelist* (Cambridge, 1945), p. 76.

[3]   *A Room of One's Own*, p. 181.

[4]   In a diary entry for April 9, 1935, Virginia Woolf recorded her passionate anger when she learned that the idea of electing a woman had been proposed and rejected at a committee meeting of the London Library. "See how my hand trembles," she wrote. "I was so angry (also very tired) standing. And I saw the whole slate smeared. I thought how perhaps M. had mentioned my name, and they had said no no no: ladies are impossible." Had she received the offer she would have rejected it, however, for she considered such a membership equivalent to having one's nose rubbed in a "pail of offal" (*A Writer's Diary*, p. 235). Aileen Pippett observes that "if anything less than the utmost was expected of her as an artist, on the grounds that she was a woman, she flew into a fury. She was prepared to do battle for other women, too, if she suspected the slightest snub, often to their surprise and embarrassment if circumstances had made them less sensitive than she to any hint of masculine condescension, any implied insult to women as a sex." *The Moth and the Star: A Biography of Virginia Woolf* (Boston, 1955), p. 12.

reverence for the masculine intellect, a reverence that did not preclude resentment, even hatred. Leslie Stephen's daughter was still struggling with the ghost of her father, that formidable old man. She was destined to vacillate all her life between defiance and a childlike desire for approval. Her father was no longer present outside her, but he remained a part of her and his voice had to be heard. If only one could reconcile the masculine, critical side of the mind with the feminine, intuitive side, light with dark—thus the problem is presented in her books. It is already the keynote in such early works as *Night and Day* (witness the title) and "The Mark on the Wall." Her novels are a kind of record of this search for wholeness; each new experiment is an attempt to embody and express this elusive unity of being. She had no single name for the ideal condition she sought, but at times she called it the androgynous mind. She was referring to a mind, as luminous as it is rare, in which masculine and feminine elements unite in perfect harmony. Her idea can be summed up in a few sentences. She had been wondering, she explained in *A Room of One's Own*,

whether there are two sexes in the mind corresponding to the two sexes in the body. . . . And in the man's brain, the man predominates over the woman, and in the woman's brain, the woman predominates over the man. The normal and comfortable state of being is that when the two live in harmony together, spiritually co-operating. If one is a man, still the woman part of the brain must have effect; and a woman also must have intercourse with the man in her. Coleridge perhaps meant this when he said that a great mind is androgynous. It is when this fusion takes place that the mind is fully fertilized and uses all its faculties. Perhaps a mind that is purely masculine cannot create, any more than a mind that is purely feminine [pp. 170-71].

In the pages that follow I shall explore her use of this idea, and the symbols related to it. For Virginia Woolf, androgyny was a kind of parable containing a solution to the dilemma of the feminist at war with herself.

The context in which the idea of androgyny first appears in *A Room of One's Own* is important. Virginia Woolf provides a narrative setting which prevents the abstraction from breaking its ties with concrete events, and which adds a dimension of feeling. What is more, her explanation is a kind of demonstration, for the idea, coming after a long feminist harangue, plays the same part in her argument as the thing itself plays in the life of the psyche: it is a resolution, it puts an end to discord.

She had been spending her days in the British Museum, she says, doing research on why women are so poor, considering the grievances of the woman writer, meditating on the new experimental novels that women were producing. She had proclaimed that they must resist the pressures of men and find the courage to be themselves at all costs. She had been bristling with indignation, when one morning a new day had dawned, and with it, instead of the impulse to take a sheet of paper and cover it with protests, had come simply a desire to look out the window. Below, she saw an ordinary London street and ordinary weekday traffic coming and going. The sight of that activity was soothing after so many days of impassioned advocacy, of keeping her mind constantly taut with argument and rebuttal, the sexes ranked like orderly troops on one side and the other. What a relief just to look out the window! Then, with echoes of strife still buzzing faintly in her head, there came a moment when everything seemed to fall still outside—even the inner buzzing grew quiet, "a complete lull and suspension of traffic."

Nothing came down the street; nobody passed. A single leaf detached itself from the plane tree at the end of the street, and in that pause and suspension fell. Somehow it was like a signal falling, a signal pointing to a force in things which one had overlooked. It seemed to point to a river, which flowed past, invisibly, round the corner, down the street, and took people and eddied them along. . . . Now it was bringing from one side of the street to the other diagonally a girl in patent leather boots, and then a young man in a maroon overcoat; it was also bringing a taxi-cab; and it brought all three together at a point directly beneath my window . . . and the girl and the young man . . . got into the taxi; and then the cab glided off as if it were swept on by the current elsewhere.

The sight was ordinary enough; what was strange was the rhythmical order with which my imagination had invested it [pp. 166–67].

Virginia Woolf was suddenly aware that what she had been doing for the past few days, thinking of "one sex as distinct from the other," had put a strain on her mind; there was something unnatural in it, and the vision of young people together in a taxi had somehow eased the tension. She reflected that this moment of harmony exemplified a higher state of mind, "a state of mind in which one could continue without effort because nothing is required to be held back," in which the undivided personality, knowing no artificial barriers, would be able to give itself wholly to the tasks that came its way. It seemed to her that there must be minds, creative minds of the highest order, for whom something like this balanced intensity was a normal condition, rather than the rare inspiration of a moment. This harmony came about, she felt certain, when the faculties within the mind did not oppose each other, intellect espousing intuition. Thus, the almost sacramental vision of the taxi-cab had led her to ask "whether there are two sexes in the mind corresponding to the two sexes in the body," and, as she put it, she had "amateurishly [sketched] a plan of the soul," the sketch of the androgynous mind quoted above. The idea of androgyny makes its appearance here as a corrective for the excesses of feminism. The opinionated mind is the very opposite of the harmonious one, a fact which is further emphasized by Virginia Woolf's choice of Shakespeare as her supreme example of an androgynous writer.

In *A Room of One's Own* Virginia Woolf, for the most part, was lecturing on freedom; in *Orlando* she indulged in it. The idea of androgyny pervades this fantasy, taking the form of a provocative confusion of the sexes. It is the only book by Virginia Woolf that evokes the sensations of physical love. Take, for instance, the episode of Orlando lying with Sasha in the snow: "Hot with skating and with love they would throw themselves down in some solitary reach, where the yellow osiers fringed the bank, and wrapped in a great fur cloak Orlando would take her in his arms, and know, for the first time, he murmured, the delights of love. Then, when the ecstasy was over and they lay lulled in a swoon on the ice, he would tell her of his other loves" (pp. 44-45). There is a kind of sensuality here that Virginia Woolf never approached elsewhere, unless, perhaps, in that crueler scene at the end of *Between the Acts* when Giles and Isa face each other: "Before they slept, they must fight; after they had fought, they would embrace. From that embrace another life might be born. But first they must fight, as the dog fox fights with the vixen. . . ." Sasha too, we recall, was like a fox, "a white Russian fox [Orlando] had had as a boy—a creature soft as snow, but with teeth of steel, which bit him so savagely that his father had it killed" (p. 44). A puzzling, extravagant book, *Orlando*; a book written in the first flush of enthusiasm, a kind of hymn to androgyny. Virginia Woolf had discovered that the barriers between the sexes could be lowered, that the sharp distinctions which wounded her like ancient taunts could be smoothed down till they lost their sting. One suspects that this was the essential liberation upon which others followed. It is especially interesting that Orlando's first, and most spectacular, change of sex is ushered in by an elaborate ritual of liberation. The scenes in which this happens contain details which cast further light on the idea of androgyny.

Orlando had been appointed Ambassador Extraordinary in Constantinople and had performed his diplomatic duties so admirably that he was awarded the Order of the Bath and elevated to a dukedom. He made these honors the occasion for a splendid entertainment in his ambassadorial mansion. In the midst of the festivities Orlando appeared on the centre Balcony, attended by

six Turks of the Imperial Body Guard, each over six foot in height . . . and a great shout went up from the people. . . . Next, Sir Adrian Scrope, in the full dress of a British Admiral advanced; the Ambassador knelt on one knee; the Admiral placed the Collar of the Most Noble Order of the Bath round his neck, then pinned the Star to his breast; after which another gentleman of the diplomatic corps advancing in a stately manner placed on his shoulders the ducal robes, and handed him on a crimson cushion, the ducal coronet [pp. 129-30].[5] Thus the proceedings were reported in the Gazette of the time. These solemnities are contrasted with a disturbance which broke out immediately thereafter. "As the coronet settled on Orlando's brows a great uproar rose. Bells began ringing; the harsh cries of the prophets were heard above the shouts of the people; many Turks fell flat to the ground and touched the earth with their foreheads" (p. 130). The total effect is to set the elaborate English ceremony against an incongruous pseudo-oriental background, and, as happens frequently in *Orlando*, to satirize the conventions of English officialdom. Furthermore, Virginia Woolf is poking fun at the rigid biographer and historian—who might have been her father—with his faith that the events recorded in newspapers and in documents contain all there is to know about history. The passage is reminiscent of the biting comments which she made on the ceremonial dress of men. The whole spectacle, in short, is a manifestation of patriarchal absurdity. It is also the first in a series of incidents leading up to the change of sex. After the disturbance has been quelled and the guests have gone home, masculine solemnities are followed by an amorous adventure. Orlando receives "a woman, much muffled, but apparently of the peasant class . . . drawn up by means of a rope . . . on to the balcony" (p. 131), and a short time later he falls into a sleep which lasts for seven days. Meanwhile, the biographer presents a ritual masque, hiding the sleeping figure from our view, and when the curtains part once again, Orlando stands revealed a woman. This masque—an interesting prelude to the change of sex

5   This passage may contain a sly allusion to a practical joke which Virginia Woolf as a young woman helped to play on the Royal Navy. Under the command of Horace Cole, "the world's champion hoaxer," she, her brother Adrian, and several others managed to pass themselves off as the Emperor of Abyssinia and his suite. Appropriately disguised, they inspected the flagship of the Channel Fleet, and got away without being discovered, even though one of the officers they passed in review happened to be Virginia and Adrian's cousin. For an account of this incident see Pippett, *The Moth and the Star*, pp. 59-63.

—represents the struggle taking place within the imaginary biographer who is both instrument and object of Virginia Woolf's satirical method. He is reluctant to record this disreputable fact, that Orlando ceased being a man and became a woman. He is torn between the demands of the austere gods, Truth, Candour, Honesty, "who keep watch and ward by the ink-pot of the biographer," and his dwarfed, official sense of propriety. Suddenly the doors open and three ghostly figures enter: "our Lady of Purity; whose brows are bound with fillets of the whitest lamb's wool . . . our lady of Chastity; on whose brow is set like a turret of burning but unwasting fire a diadem of icicles . . . [and] our Lady of Modesty . . . whose face is only shown as the young moon shows when it is thin and sickle shaped and half hidden among clouds" (p. 134). The three figures plead for secrecy; the struggle intensifies, but they are powerless to prevent the revelation, and Truth, with a flourish of trumpets, banishes these champions of propriety, one by one. But before they relinquish the field, they join once again to invoke the powers that protect and cherish them.

"We go; we go. I *(Purity says this)* to the hen roost. I *(Chastity says this)* to the still unravished heights of Surrey. I *(Modesty says this)* to any cosy nook where there are curtains in plenty.

"For there . . . dwell still in nest and boudoir, office and lawcourt those who love us; those who honour us, virgins and city men; lawyers and doctors; those who prohibit; those who deny; those who reverence without knowing why . . . the still very numerous . . . tribe of the respectable; who prefer to see not . . . love the darkness; those still worship us, and with reason; for we have given them Wealth, Prosperity, Comfort, Ease" [pp. 136–37].

The doors having closed upon these sisters, Orlando wakes. "He stood upright in complete nakedness before us, and . . . we have no choice left but confess—he was a woman." Thus the liberation is accomplished. Purity, Chastity, Modesty, who are allied with the repressive forces of "boudoir, office, lawcourt," with "virgins, city men, lawyers, doctors," have been exorcised. The truth of androgyny that releases from the bondage of the intellect plays lightly upon scene after scene, turning everything into fantasy. Virginia Woolf is able to take the liberty of showing us Orlando without clothes on. "Orlando stood stark naked," she repeats. "No human being, since the world began, has ever looked more ravishing" (p. 138). It is a refreshing novelty to find Virginia Woolf looking at a naked body and enjoying it. But there is a serious intention behind her playfulness. This whole sequence—the pompous ceremony, which shows Orlando in the clutches of patriarchal vanity, the riot which disturbs it, the furtive love affair, the seven-day sleep, and the final exorcism—illustrates a movement from repression to freedom. There is serious meaning, too, in the words with which Virginia Woolf describes the "tribe of the respectable," who would rather not know of the change of sex, who shield themselves behind "Wealth, Prosperity, Comfort, Ease." A note of bitterness is distinctly audible. And her words here about chastity may be compared with her reflections on the same subject in *Three Guineas*, where she protested that chastity is a false ideal, twisting the minds of women, playing havoc with their instincts, an instrument of oppression. Chastity is a masculine invention, traceable to St. Paul. It is a "complex conception," she wrote, founded, "subconsciously, upon a very strong and natural desire that the woman's mind and body shall be reserved for the use of one man and one only" (p. 298). The banishment of Chastity and her attendant graces is accompanied by the throwing off of rational restraints which ordinarily keep a work of fiction within certain fixed limits. So effectively are the barriers broken down that we have the greatest difficulty in knowing how to refer to *Orlando*; it does not fit into any of the established categories. Fantasy, novel, biography, poem, history —all of these terms may be applied to the book, but no single one describes it adequately. It seems fitting that this book about the intermingling of the sexes should be a hybrid of several literary types.

Orlando's dramatic change of sex is only a single manifestation, however, of a fact which had been established much earlier. Orlando is androgynous from the beginning, as the opening sentence of the book hints. Now, changed into a woman, he "combined in one the strength of a man and a woman's grace." But the change has had to do with externals, with accidents, not with essences. "In every other respect Orlando remained precisely as he had been" (p. 138). The outer change is, as it were, a parable of an inner reality which is always present. "Different though the sexes are," Virginia Woolf observes, "they intermix. In every human being a vacillation from one sex to the other takes place, and often it is only the clothes that keep the male or female likeness, while underneath the sex is the very opposite of what it is above" (p. 189). This intermixing of sexes, and the consequent ambiguity, is observable in several characters. Sasha, the Russian Princess, at first appears to be a boy and later dresses as a man. The Archduchess Harriet reveals that she has only been masquerading as a woman. But she is not androgynous at all, in the ideal sense, because the masculine element has always predominated in her, even before her dropping of the feminine disguise brought inner and outer sexes into conformity with each other. The portrait of the Archduke is drawn in a rare mood of compassion for the shortcomings of the one-sided male, although the poor man is guilty of nearly killing Orlando with boredom. His masculine heavy-handedness reduces them both to whiling away hours playing fly loo; and their talk is confined to sterile formalities.[6] Orlando, and her husband Shelmardine, on the other hand, are truly androgynous, the two sexes within them almost evenly balanced. It is because of the fineness of this balance that Orlando must constantly be shifting back and forth, that is, conforming her outer sex to changes in the inner weather. For the dramatic

[6] Constance Hunting holds that the Archduke's nature is "essentially feminine," and his attraction to Orlando a lesbian one, but while she acknowledges that the Archduke remains masculine in body, even when he is dressed as a woman, and that he is "appropriately an enthusiast of hunting, horse-racing and gambling," she gives no convincing evidence in support of her contention that he "remains feminine in personality." See "Technique in *Orlando*," *Modern Fiction Studies*, 2 (February, 1956): 22. There seems no reason to maintain an opinion in direct contradiction to the Archduke's testimony that "he was a man and always had been one" (p. 179).

change of sex is only the first of many changes that follow
without fanfare. The state of things becomes apparent shortly
after Orlando's transformation into a woman. The narrator
finds that Orlando "was censuring both sexes equally, as if
she belonged to neither; and indeed, for the time being she
seemed to vacillate; she was man; she was woman; she knew
the secrets, shared the weaknesses of each. It was a most
bewildering and whirligig state of mind to be in" (p. 158).
Nevertheless, as James Hafley observes, Orlando

can achieve a balance of intellect and intuition possible only in
a fantasy. . . . The mentally androgynous man and woman can
understand each other with a perfection impossible to those
barred behind the limitations of their sex. When Orlando and
Marmaduke meet, they understand each other immediately:
"An awful suspicion rushed into both their minds simultaneously.
     'You're a woman, Shel!' she cried.
     'You're a man, Orlando!' he cried.
The truth is that both are androgynous. . . . To be only a
man in mind or only a woman . . . is to be hopelessly isolated
and to perish. [Thus, Orlando's final self-realization] is not
possible until her husband (who drops from an airplane) joins
her.[7]

The aim of the book, Hafley concludes, is to record Orlando's
joining of the two sides of her nature in perfect harmony, so
that she attains truth, the symbolic wild goose, and becomes
"a real woman," that is, perfectly androgynous.[8]

[7]   *The Glass Roof: Virginia Woolf as Novelist* (Berkeley, 1954),
     p. 104. Cf. Hafley's statement that "Orlando, by becoming a
     woman, adds intuitive to intellectual knowledge, and the gradual
     development of that intuitive faculty leads her to her final
     perception of réality" (p. 103). The whole discussion of the idea
     of androgyny (pp. 101–5) is most valuable.
[8]   Androgynous characters are not, of course, confined to *Orlando*.
     As Winifred Holtby points out, "Mrs. Woolf . . . makes her . . .
     characters manly-womanly and womanly-manly. Her women
     may not all have been men once, as Orlando was, but they
     harbour a hidden man in their hearts. Thus, though the sexes
     differ, they do not estrange. Once inside the taxi of human
     personality, man and woman can instruct each other." *Virginia
     Woolf* (London, 1932), p. 182. Occasionally in her novels Virginia
     continued on next page

The first use to which Virginia Woolf put her idea of androgyny after formulating it in *A Room of One's Own* was as a critical tool. The idea illuminated the problems of the woman writer. It explained, moreover, why so much of the fiction currently being written by men seemed unsatisfactory to a woman. For Mr. Galsworthy, Mr. Kipling, were guilty of "writing only with the male side of their brains" (p. 176). "Neither . . . has a spark of the woman in him. Thus all their qualities seem to a woman . . . crude and immature. They lack suggestive power" (p. 178). These were the modern masters of fiction whom young writers were encouraged to emulate. In truth, Virginia Woolf's whole criticism of the Edwardian novel, as a careful reading of her essay, "Mr. Bennett and Mrs. Brown," shows, came down to this: that the novelists were one-sided; that they were writing with the masculine side of their minds only. Like the critic, Mr. B., mentioned in *A Room of One's Own*, who wrote so acutely, but so unpoetically, of poetry, their "feelings no longer communicated; [their minds] seemed separated into different chambers; not a sound carried from one to the other" (p. 176). "A mind that is purely masculine," she had said, "cannot create, any more than a mind that is purely

---

[8] *continued*

   Woolf explicitly says that a character combines feminine and masculine traits. These instances reveal no particular pattern (no doubt she considered characters androgynous without specifically saying so), but they do prove that she had the idea of androgyny in mind throughout her career, and as early as *The Voyage Out*. In this novel, we find Mrs. Dalloway describing her husband, surprisingly enough, as "man and woman as well" (p. 61). And Evelyn comments that there's "something of a woman" in Terence (p. 247). More significantly, in *Night and Day* Virginia Woolf tells us that Katharine and Cassandra "represented very well the manly and the womanly sides of the feminine nature" (p. 341). The statement is supported by an association between Katharine and Shakespeare's Rosalind. (See pp. 175, 306.) In *To the Lighthouse*, speaking of the Ramsay girls, she alludes to "the manliness in their girlish hearts" (p. 14). Finally, in *The Waves*, Bernard, inventing his own biography, observes that "joined to the sensibility of a woman . . . [he] possessed the logical sobriety of a man" (p. 55).

feminine."[9] A not very different thought lies behind the little parable of Mrs. Brown in Virginia Woolf's essay. In order to depict the dilemma of the modern novelist, she tells of an incident she observed during a rail trip, and of an anonymous woman whom she christened Mrs. Brown. Mrs. Brown sat opposite her, emanating that mysterious essence, character. "The impression she made was overwhelming. It came pouring out like a draught, like a smell of burning."[10] It started one making up stories about her, almost compelled one to begin writing a novel. Virginia Woolf now imagined what would have happened had Wells, Galsworthy, and Bennett been riding in the railway carriage. The first two, instead of trying to seize that ineffable substance, would have fixed their eyes on the passing landscape outside the window —Wells, to depict a Utopia beyond the pane, Galsworthy, to describe the plight of workers in a factory. Only Arnold Bennett would have kept his eyes inside the carriage, but, instead of trying to capture the essence of Mrs. Brown, he would have busied himself in describing what Mrs. Brown was wearing, the railway advertisements, the upholstery of the seats. No more than the other two could he be counted on to carry out his duties as a novelist. "He is trying to make us imagine for him," Virginia Woolf protested; "He is trying to hypnotize us into the belief that, because he has made a house, there must be a person living there" (p. 103). Reflecting on the works of this triumvirate, she exclaims: "What odd books they are! Sometimes I wonder if we are right to call them books at all. For they leave one with so strange a feeling of incompleteness and dissatisfaction. In order to complete them it seems necessary to do something —to join a society, or, more desperately, to write a cheque" (p. 99). A great book, however, causes no such restlessness or frustration; it is complete in itself, whole. Admirable as these writers are, none of them has succeeded in capturing Mrs. Brown, and "Mrs. Brown is eternal, Mrs. Brown is human nature" (p. 103). Reflecting on Mrs. Brown, on the failure

[9] See p. 108, above.
[10] In *The Captain's Death Bed*, pp. 95–96.

of these novelists, on the odd feeling of incompleteness and dissatisfaction with which, if what Virginia Woolf says is true, they leave the reader, one's mind goes back to the incident in the railway carriage that originally brought Mrs. Brown before us. Mrs. Brown had not been alone at first, when Virginia Woolf entered the carriage; she had been in the company of a burly, powerful man in his forties. Observing them, it had become plain to Virginia Woolf that the man was bullying the little old lady, forcing her to do something against her will. That was the incident that had first attracted Virginia Woolf's attention and made her particularly conscious of the old lady's emanations, after the man had departed and Mrs. Brown had been left alone, "suffering intensely." The little old lady stands for "human nature," but also, perhaps, for the English novel; she is being bullied by the burly man as the woman writer is bullied by the male novelist.[11] And, of course, the bully is blind to his own shortcomings. That is precisely what Bennett, Galsworthy, and Wells were doing, according to Virginia Woolf—blindly imposing upon the novel a standard derived from a one-sidedly masculine view of the world. "The writer seems constrained," she wrote elsewhere, ". . . by some powerful and unscrupulous tyrant who has him in thrall, to provide a plot, to provide comedy, tragedy, love, interest, and an air of probability embalming the whole so impeccable that if all his figures were to come to life they would find themselves dressed down to the last button of their coats in the fashion of the hour."[12]

Virginia Woolf's quarrel, then, with the Edwardian novelists, and her somewhat grudging defense of the Georgians, was based on the fact that the Edwardians were masculine chauvinists, exponents of one-sidedness, who believed with Mr. Bennett that characters in a novel "ought to be made of freehold villas and copyhold estates, not of

[11]   In the opening sentence of a review of E. M. Forster's *Aspects of the Novel*, Virginia Woolf wrote that "fiction is a lady and a lady who has somehow got herself into trouble." "The Art of Fiction," *The Moment*, p. 89.

[12]   "Modern Fiction," *The Common Reader* (1st ser.), pp. 211–12.

imagination,"[13] while the Georgians were struggling to restore the balance, to write of the higher life. The Edwardian novelists were materialists, she charged in "Modern Fiction"; "Mr. Joyce [on the other hand] is spiritual; he is concerned at all costs to reveal the flickerings of that innermost flame which flashes its messages through the brain."[14] Joyce was aware, unlike Bennett, Galsworthy, Wells, that life is composed of something more than externals; he was striving to capture the whole of experience, not just a part. To do so, for Virginia Woolf, meant to succeed in illuminating the data supplied by the intellect with the light of intuition, to attain to the andrygynous mind.

The Georgians were performing necessary tasks of destruction, clearing away debris that stood in the way of progress, but they had achieved only limited success artistically. In freeing themselves from the clutches of literary convention they had fallen into another trap, one similar to that which awaits the woman writer: they could not stop reacting. They had not been able to achieve the steady vision of the artist who keeps his eye on the object, unaffected by ulterior motives, having no axe to grind, no grievances to protest. Virginia Woolf interpreted Joyce's "obscenity" and Eliot's "obscurity" as overreactions against the extreme one-sidedness of Edwardian literature.

> The literary convention of the time is so artificial [she wrote]
> . . . that, naturally, the feeble are tempted to outrage, and the
> strong are led to destroy the very foundations and rules of
> literary society. Signs of this are everywhere apparent. Grammar
> is violated; syntax disintegrated; as a boy staying with an aunt
> for the week-end rolls in the geranium bed out of sheer
> desperation as the solemnities of the sabbath wear on.[15]

Joyce's and Eliot's efforts were admirable, but the extremes of banality and confusion against which they were reacting had ultimately taken their toll. "Their sincerity is desperate, and their courage tremendous; it is only that they do not

---

13   *The Captain's Death Bed*, p. 107.
14   *The Common Reader* (1st ser.), p. 214.
15   "Mr. Bennett and Mrs. Brown," *The Captain's Death Bed*, p. 108.

know which to use, a fork or their fingers. . . . Mr. Joyce's indecency in *Ulysses* seems to me the conscious and calculated indecency of a desperate man who feels that in order to breathe he must break the windows. At moments, when the window is broken, he is magnificent. But what a waste of energy!"[16] As long as writers found themselves divided from society as a whole, and forced to spend so much of their time joining battle on side issues, rather than being able to devote all their gifts to the perfection of their art, readers would have to reconcile themselves "to a season of failures and fragments. We must reflect that where so much strength is spent on finding a way of telling the truth, the truth itself is bound to reach us in rather an exhausted and chaotic condition."[17]

The woman novelist shared the problems common to the practitioners of her art, as well as inheriting problems peculiar to her sex. Women writers had always given undue weight to masculine claims, Virginia Woolf believed. Either they had tried to write exactly as men write, to adopt a style essentially foreign to them, or they had tried to write as men expect women to write.[18] In the one case they had created skillful parodies of the masculine style that would not, however, stand comparison with the originals; in the other case they had concocted an artificial feminine manner that did little more than flatter the bias of those who believed in the inferiority of women. Only a handful of women writers had succeeded in shaping styles of their own, not patterned upon alien models. As Virginia Woolf saw it, the writing of women, when they discovered their own mode of expression, would differ essentially from that of men, but it would have as little in common with the sentimental style often identified as "feminine" as did the work of Jane Austen and Emily Brontë. Women would reshape the fundamental unit, the

[16]   *Ibid.*, pp. 108-9.
[17]   *Ibid.*, p. 110.
[18]   In a review of *The Women Novelists* by R. Brimley Johnson, Virginia Woolf observed that "the women who wished to be taken for men in what they wrote were certainly common enough; and if they have given place to the women who wish to be taken for women, the change is hardly for the better." "Women Novelists," *TLS*, October 17, 1918, p. 495.

sentence, so as to adapt it to their own purposes, for the sentence current in nineteenth-century fiction, for instance, was "a man's sentence" and "unsuited for a woman's use. Charlotte Brontë, with all her splendid gift for prose, stumbled and fell with that clumsy weapon in her hands. George Eliot committed atrocities with it that beggar description. Jane Austen looked at it and laughed at it and devised a perfectly natural, shapely sentence proper for her own use and never departed from it."[19] Similarly, the values prevailing in current fiction were values which had been "made by the other sex. . . . Speaking crudely, football and sport are 'important'; the worship of fashion, the buying of clothes 'trivial.'"[20] And the efforts of women to adjust to these alien values, like their efforts to use the masculine sentence, had deformed many a work of fiction. The very substance of the novel was destined to change in their hands as they began to describe life from their own special angle. Hitherto, women characters had been seen almost exclusively in their relations to men; necessarily, vast areas of experience had been excluded from the fictional record. "Suppose, for instance," Virginia Woolf mused, "that men were only represented in literature as the lovers of women, and were never the friends of men, soldiers, thinkers, dreamers; how few parts in the plays of Shakespeare could be allotted to them."[21] Women novelists were destined to explore this all but virgin territory, and in doing so, to shape a literary form more suited to their use than the novel of the present, with its masculine bias.

It was impossible to predict precisely what shape the creations of the androgynous mind would take; probably they would differ from anything that had gone before. But Virginia Woolf could already detect the first halting steps toward freedom; important changes were under way. In *A Room of One's Own*, in order to express her ideas on these changes, she invented Mary Carmichael, a young writer who had just published her first novel, *Life's Adventure*. Mary Carmichael was by no means an accomplished artist; she was

19   *A Room of One's Own*, p. 133.
20   *Ibid.*, p. 128.
21   *Ibid.*, pp. 144–45.

a struggling novice. But, having been born late enough to benefit from the emancipation of women, she had been able to clear some hurdles that had tripped up her predecessors. She had been able to ignore "the bishops and the deans, the doctors and the professors, the patriarchs and the pedagogues all at her shouting warning and advice. You can't do this and you shan't do that" (p. 163). Having passed this hurdle, she was beginning to make her way along the unfamiliar path. Taking up her novel with intense curiosity, Virginia Woolf noticed almost at once that Mary had deviated from conventional novelistic technique in two ways. She had broken the sentence; she had tampered with the expected sequence. This new novelist had rejected Jane Austen's sentence in favor of a remarkable "terseness . . . short-windedness," as if she were "afraid of being called 'sentimental' perhaps," or as if she remembered "that women's writing has been called flowery and so [provided] a superfluity of thorns" (p. 140). She had failed, moreover, to provide what is usually expected by way of a plot. Instead, she had substituted quite unnovelistic observations, scenes having nothing to do with romantic love, war, sport, or intrigue. "Cloe liked Olivia," she had written. "They shared a laboratory together" (p. 144). She was beginning to exercise her new freedom by writing of the whole of experience, and writing of it as a woman. She was bringing to light areas of life that had never been exposed before. Obviously, in order for her experiments to succeed, her mind must be free, as well as her person. Her road toward fulfilment as an artist led from the familiar feminist demands toward androgyny. That broken sentence, that shift in sequence were, for Virginia Woolf, important signs of progress toward the goal. They were symbolic of inner changes.

Now if Chloe likes Olivia and they share a laboratory, which of itself will make their friendship more varied and lasting because it will be less personal; if Mary Carmichael knows how to write, and I was beginning to enjoy some quality in her style; if she has a room to herself, of which I am not quite sure; if she has five hundred a year of her own—but that remains to be proved —then I think that something of great importance has happened

For if Chloe likes Olivia and Mary Carmichael knows how to express it she will light a torch in that vast chamber where nobody has yet been. It is all half lights and profound shadows like those serpentine caves where one goes with a candle peering up and down [pp. 145–46].

Here Virginia Woolf sketches the movement toward liberation, as far as it has gone: the personal freedom that makes it possible for Mary Carmichael to be an artist; the economic independence that enables her to make use of her freedom; the ability to see women in relation to each other; the struggle to find a new style appropriate to new subject matter; the opening of hitherto obscure regions of women's minds. Undoubtedly, the illumination of the cavern, the increase in self-knowledge, would bring women one step closer to androgyny. Finally, there is the significance of Virginia Woolf's style in this passage; her thoughts are expressed in a poetic language relatively free of abstractions, a language that weds idea to feeling. The above passage may perhaps itself be proposed as a fair example of the workings of the androgynous mind.

The final test of whether or not an artist is approaching the ideal state of androgyny is his objectivity: can he keep his attention whole and undivided upon his artistic object? In the case of women writers it follows that one can almost measure their greatness by the extent to which they have managed to forget their grievances.

What genius, what integrity it must have required [Virginia Woolf observes of nineteenth-century women writers] . . . in the midst of that purely patriarchal society, to hold fast to the thing as they saw it without shrinking. Only Jane Austen did it and Emily Brontë. It is another feather, perhaps the finest, in their caps. They wrote as women write, not as men write. Of all the thousand women who wrote novels then, they alone entirely ignored the perpetual admonitions of the eternal pedagogue.[22]

22 *Ibid.*, pp. 129–30. Cf. the passage in *The Voyage Out*, where Virginia Woolf puts similar sentiments about the virtues of Jane Austen into the mouth of Richard Dalloway: "She is incomparably the greatest female writer we possess," the politician asserts ". . . and for this reason: she does not attempt to write like a man. Every other woman does" (p. 62).

Their minds had become luminous, incandescent; no indignation destroyed the clarity, no self-consciousness clouded the purity, of their vision.

2

Virginia Woolf saw the universe as the scene of an eternal conflict between opposites, corresponding, roughly speaking, to masculine and feminine principles. Her main concern was to find ways of reconciling the warring opposites. As a practical feminist she sought equality between the sexes, a dynamic balance between the two halves of mankind which would lead to social regeneration. As artist and mystic she sought inner harmony, the ideal state of androgyny, which would lead to the renewal of the individual. Psychic freedom must wait on political freedom, however, for how could women achieve harmony until they were free of a sense of grievance? One might say that, for Virginia Woolf, feminism and mysticism converged in the doctrine of androgyny. This view of reality was the keynote of her novels; they demonstrated the war of opposites. In her early stories she dealt mainly with social problems: young men and women found it difficult to marry. In her later work she dealt with psychic problems: the individual found it difficult to reconcile masculine and feminine sides of himself.

This view of her work is at least partially corroborated by a consensus of the critics. Virginia Woolf's books, they agree, are marked by a striking dualism. Most of them consider the tendency to unite disparate elements one of the most important characteristics of her style. David Daiches, for instance, finds an antithesis in the novels "between the city and the shore, between London and Cornwall. . . . One might even push the symbolic contrast further and see an opposition between reason, London, and her paternal heredity on the one hand, and intuition, Cornwall, and the legacy of her mother's family on the other. The combination of these two sets of opposites produced her unique kind of vision."[23]

[23] *Virginia Woolf* (Norfolk, Conn., 1942), p. 3.

Victoria Sackville-West, in a reminiscence of her friend, associates Virginia Woolf with the androgynous Coleridge. "She and Coleridge both seem to me to combine the unusually mixed ingredients of genius and intellect, the wild, fantastic intuitive genius on the one hand, and the cold, reasoning intellect on the other."[24] Bernard Blackstone finds her work pervaded by "the antithesis of reason and intuition," and James Hafley devotes many pages to this antithesis in his penetrating analysis of the novels.[25] Winifred Holtby detects "two streams of thought—one practical, controversial, analytical; the other creative, poetical, audacious."[26] Ralph Freedman writes that Virginia Woolf "noted an almost classical dualism, extending from the relationship of mind and body to the philosophically distinct relations between self-consciousness and its world."[27] To her biographer, Virginia Woolf appears to be "a woman divided against herself, desiring but never achieving an unattainable unity."[28] Related points of view are presented in two further summaries

[24]   *Horizon*, 3, no. 17 (May, 1941): 321.
[25]   Bernard Blackstone, *Virginia Woolf: A Commentary* (New York, 1949), p. 26. Cf. *The Glass Roof*, p. 108 and *passim*.
[26]   *Virginia Woolf*, p. 200.
[27]   "Awareness and Fact: The Lyrical Vision of Virginia Woolf," in *The Lyrical Novel* (Princeton, 1963), p. 198.
[28]   *The Moth and the Star*, p. 286. Several other writers comment in similar terms on these opposing tendencies. Floris Delattre writes: "C'est ce double aspect: grâce féminine et indépendance intellectuelle . . . c'est cette combinaison de discipline ancienne, toujours si délicatement nuancée, et de rébellion moderne, aux mouvements si hardis; c'est le jeu alterné de la diversité et de l'unité, le conflit même de l'obscur et du clair qui constituent l'originalité de la personnalité littéraire de Virginia Woolf." *Le Roman psychologique de Virginia Woolf* (Paris, 1932), p. 2. William Plomer observes that "in each of us there are two beings, one solitary and one social. . . . In Virginia the two beings had an equal life and so made her a complete person. The two beings can be perceived in her writings, sometimes distinct, sometimes merged. The special genius of her rare and solitary spirit reached its purest expression in *The Waves*. . . . The social being in Virginia, the novelist, can be seen most essentially not in her fiction but in *The Common Reader*." *Horizon*, 3 (May, 1941): 325. Joan Bennett

continued on next page

of her work. Edwin Berry Burgum observes that "the recurrent theme of her fiction . . . is the loss in the modern world of the Renaissance ideal of the well-rounded man, what our psychology terms the man of well-integrated personality."[29] Virginia Woolf undoubtedly would have added that the most striking characteristic of such an "integrated personality" is its androgynous nature. Finally, in describing the conflict between "inner" and "outer" in *Night and Day*, Dorothy Brewster writes that "to bring inner and outer into harmony is the aim of many of Virginia Woolf's experiments in technique; and this harmony, when achieved at rare moments, is the perfect flowing together of the stream of consciousness and the stream of events. It is symbolized by one of her favorite images, that of the globe, which 'we spend our lives trying to shape, round, whole and entire from the confusion of chaos.' "[30] We may refer, once again, to Virginia Woolf's own testimony in *A Room of One's Own* that "some collaboration has to take place in the mind between the woman and the man before the act of creation can be accomplished. Some marriage of opposites has to be consummated" (p. 181).

Virginia Woolf's description of the ideal state of being that resulted from a marriage of opposites was necessarily vague. She could say little more about androgyny in *A Room of One's Own* than that it existed. But as a novelist she sought and found symbolic equivalents for the androgynous mind. A brief review of the themes of three novels will illustrate some of her attempts to "bring inner and outer into harmony" and clear the way for a more detailed discussion of her use of symbolism.

Night and Day, To the Lighthouse and *The Years* provide examples of different ways in which Virginia Woolf arrived

[28] *continued*
    notices "a peculiar conflict or tension of the mind, as of one poised between two opposed beliefs." *Virginia Woolf: Her Art as a Novelist*, p. 65. And Ruth Gruber finds that she "sees all things, like a Noah's ark, in pairs." *Virginia Woolf: A Study* (Leipzig, 1935), p. 77.
[29]   *The Novel and the World's Dilemma* (New York, 1947), p. 123.
[30]   *Virginia Woolf's London* (New York, 1960), p. 30.

at ideal solutions to the problem of the opposites. Of the three, *Night and Day* is most concerned with externals. As we have already observed, the title alludes to a conflict between solitude and society, between conventional outer life and the inner life of the individual. Furthermore, we have seen that Virginia Woolf identified convention with the masculine principle; in *Night and Day* she made the one-sided character, William Rodney, place propriety ahead of all other considerations. Katharine Hilbery and Ralph Denham, for their part, might have, but did not, fall into the trap of rejecting convention altogether. To do so would have meant exchanging one kind of one-sidedness for another. Instead, they resolved to combine the opposites in an experimental marriage. There is some possibility that they will succeed. Katharine and Ralph, Virginia Woolf implies, are both essentially androgynous; each one combines the opposites within his own personality. But they are both vividly aware that a cleavage still exists between their practical lives and their dreams. To put it another way, the function of their marriage, both as symbol and as reality, is to enable them to complete each other, to help each other perfect their androgyneity.

In *To the Lighthouse*, the wholeness, the completeness, of Mrs. Ramsay stands in sharp contrast to the one-sidedness of the other characters. Mrs. Ramsay as wife, mother, hostess, is the androgynous artist in life, creating with the whole of her being. Compared to the harmony she has created, both Mr. Ramsay's treatises and Lily Briscoe's paintings seem paltry things. After death, Mrs. Ramsay becomes a symbol of wholeness toward which Lily and Mr. Ramsay sail. There are, in effect, two Mrs. Ramsays: the living woman who, in spite of the tremendous force of her personality, shares the weaknesses of other mortals, and the perfect symbolic figure toward whom her husband and her friend turn in aspiration as toward a liberating ideal. Comparing *Night and Day* and *To the Lighthouse* as solutions to the conflict of opposites, we might say that the first proposes an ideal way of life, while the second presents an ideal personality. And *The Years*, we might add, describes an ideal state of consciousness, a mystical vision.

Once again, the resolution has to do with the perfecting of the androgynous mind, for Eleanor's vision at the end of the novel, though sufficiently occult, clearly is related to androgyny. That vision, we recall, is in reality composed of two parts: in the first, Eleanor drifts into a dream-state of happiness while clutching coins which are associated with the core of the self; in the second, she looks out of the window and finds deep meaning in the sight of a young man and woman coming home in a taxi at dawn. Both experiences give her a sense of liberation, and the similarity of the latter to the taxi scene in *A Room of One's Own* need hardly be pointed out. But in becoming part of a human drama, the discovery of androgyny in *The Years* gains a dimension that was lacking in the earlier book. Eleanor, having descended to the core of the self (an achievement symbolized by her dream and the coins), grasps the possibility of joining opposing elements in the mind into a harmonious whole. A little later the vision is reaffirmed in the outer world by a sight that echoes the inner revelation. Even nature seems to be giving its benediction.

Night and Day, To the Lighthouse, The Years—typical early, middle, and late novels—illustrate a progression in Virginia Woolf's works from external to internal, from practical to mystical, in spite of the apparent increase of interest in mundane affairs. The sense of conflict, and the search for liberation through a marriage of opposites remain constant factors, but the dramas themselves take place on different levels. Mere changes in social life, which were to bring about harmony in *Night and Day*, are seen to be of dubious value in *To the Lighthouse* (Lily Briscoe's philosophy and way of life are forward-looking, Mrs. Ramsay's outmoded, but the former is certainly no improvement upon the latter, as Katharine Hilbery's views were an improvement upon those of her mother), and in *The Years* we learn that harmony, if it can be achieved at all, must be almost purely subjective, based on an inner vision. Virginia Woolf seems to have had less and less faith, as the years went by, in external solutions to problems which she came to regard as primarily spiritual.

A great deal of the symbolism in Virginia Woolf's novels

is related to this search for wholeness (we have discussed some instances: man and woman against the sky, "taxi of personality") and it forms a fairly consistent pattern, bridging the gap between the early and later works. Let us begin with an early story published in 1917. When examined with the idea of androgyny in mind, "The Mark on the Wall" proves to be more than the mere stream of random associations that some critics have taken it to be. One can clearly trace the workings here of the mind that imagined the taxi scenes in *A Room of One's Own* and *The Years*. The pattern that was to be decisive in the later work had already taken shape.

The story consists almost entirely of the late afternoon meditations of a lady seated in the drawing room of her house. She has noticed a mark on the wall above her mantelpiece, but cannot determine, from this distance, what kind of mark it is. Disinclined to move, she sits turning over the sudden apparition in her mind. But her mind starts wandering to the former occupants of the house, the uncertainty of life; how fugitive solid objects are, she reflects, we have no control, we lose things, our feeble attempts at order are frustrated, and life resembles "being blown through the Tube at fifty miles an hour—landing at the other end without a single hairpin in one's hair! Shot out at the feet of God entirely naked!"[31] These are the first notes of discord. She sees a meaningless universe, composed, somehow, of God and hairpins, of meadows of asphodel and brown paper parcels. Her mind rambles on, apparently at random, but only apparently. Slowly, the discord begins to resolve itself into a more or less orderly conflict between two opposing principles, one associated with the world of imagination, the other with the world of fact. The idea of God has made her contemplate the afterlife, where "there will be nothing but spaces of light and dark, intersected by thick stalks, and rather higher up perhaps, rose-shaped blots of an indistinct colour —dim pinks and blues" (p. 42). This world has an almost hypnotic fascination for her, and she wants, she says, "to sink

---

[31]   *A Haunted House*, p. 41. All the following passages from "The Mark on the Wall" are quoted from this collection.

deeper and deeper, away from the surface, with its hard separate facts." She can't quite do it, sink away from the surface. "The tree outside the window taps very gently on the pane." Caught between the two worlds, each of which seems to contradict the other, she searches for something intermediate between the two. "To steady myself, let me catch hold of the first idea that passes. . . . Shakespeare. . . . Well, he will do as well as another. A man who sat himself solidly in an arm-chair, and looked into the fire, so—A shower of ideas fell perpetually from some very high Heaven down through his mind" (p. 42). Significantly, it is Shakespeare, the man of luminous mind, who is her symbol of reconciliation, combining the opposites, sitting "solidly in an arm-chair," while opening his mind to a "shower of ideas . . . from some very high Heaven." But the idea of Shakespeare is not powerful enough to dispel the discord, perhaps because it is not based on anything immediate that she can see and touch. "How dull this is, this historical fiction!" she protests. "It doesn't interest me at all." And her mind slowly drifts back. She finds herself embroiled in the conflict once again.

Now she is thinking that there are two levels of reality: that of the inner self, represented by a reflection in a mirror, a "romantic figure with the green of forest depths all about it," and that of the outer shell, the world of appearances, "airless, shallow, bald"; and the two worlds, of course, exist side by side. "As we face each other in omnibuses and underground railways we are looking into the mirror" (p. 43). Virginia Woolf is disposed to favor the inner world. "The novelists in future," she muses, "will realize more and more the importance of these reflections . . . those are the depths they will explore, those the phantoms they will pursue, leaving the description of reality more and more out of their stories." But having inclined rather far to one side, she suddenly finds herself swinging back in the opposite direction, caught up by the word "reality." "The military sound of the word is enough," she realizes. "It recalls leading articles, cabinet ministers—a whole class of things indeed which, as a child, one thought the thing itself, the standard thing, the real thing, from which one could not depart save at the risk of nameless damnation" (p. 44). The mention of "leading articles, cabinet ministers," points to an association between the world of facts she has been writing about and the masculine principle. The connection becomes still more marked as the narrator's thoughts pass to the patriarchal world of her childhood, a world of order, a world of rules, of "Sunday luncheons, Sunday walks, country houses," a world that even set strict standards to govern the choice of tablecloths. The passage culminates in a question that can leave no doubt as to her meaning. "What now takes the place of those things I wonder, those real standard things? Men perhaps, should you be a woman; the masculine point of view which governs our lives... which established Whitaker's Table of Precedency" (p. 44). Lately, she goes on to point out, the patriarchy has been losing its hold, although its standards are still so deeply ingrained that its liberated slaves experience, not real release, but "an intoxicating sense of illegitimate freedom." And the mention of freedom causes her mind to pause in its wandering; her thoughts return to the mark on the wall. For she has in reality been circling, all the while, round that mysterious starting point, drifting back toward it as toward a center. And we begin now to perceive the power of the mark on the wall to resolve, or to surmount, the conflict, to remove the mind that contemplates it beyond the realm of contradictions altogether.

This power of the mark on the wall becomes clearer a little further on, as the conflict once again begins to intensify, and the narrator sits imagining a utopian retreat into a feminine world "without professors or specialists . . . a world which one could slice with one's thought as a fish slices the water with his fin. . . . How peaceful it is down here, rooted in the centre of the world . . . if it were not for Whitaker's Almanack —if it were not for the Table of Precedency" (p. 46). Thus, as ever, the masculine order intrudes, breaking in upon her most entrancing dreams. But just as she is about to fall into a rage, finally to give vent to her anger at this round of frustrations, her thoughts, as if of themselves, revert to the mark on the wall, distracting her, saving her. And she realizes that

it is "nature . . . at her old game of self-preservation." For
nature knows that it is foolish, perhaps even dangerous, to
come into collision with "reality." Nature counsels her not
to rebel uselessly, and, if she cannot help herself, to stop her
"disagreeable thoughts by looking at a mark on the wall."
"Indeed," she affirms, "now that I have fixed my eyes upon
it, I feel that I have grasped a plank in the sea; I feel a satisfying sense of reality which at once turns the two Archbishops
and the Lord High Chancellor to the shadows of shades"
(p. 47). Although there is no way of denying the reality of
"facts" and the masculine order, it is possible to transcend
them, to penetrate to a higher reality, freeing oneself from
conflict, achieving wholeness. The symbol of integration, the
mark on the wall, we discover in the last sentence, is a snail,
a living thing that may be said to combine the opposites
within itself—the shell, the hard, inanimate outer structure
protecting and concealing a dark, evasive living center.[32] It
is because the mark on the wall as symbol embraces both
aspects, world of fact and world of imagination, that the
narrator has a sense of being enlarged and set free when she
contemplates it.

The pattern traced in "The Mark on the Wall" is repeated
in various ways in Virginia Woolf's novels, though the
central symbol has been changed. In the longer works it is the
lighthouse (and a cluster of related images) that plays the part
assigned to the snail in the early story. Like the mark on the
wall, it becomes a symbolic equivalent for the idea of
androgyny. In discussing the lighthouse image, I shall understand the term to include any radiant source emitting
pulsations of light into the darkness, rising enisled in the midst

32 The snail is also used in *The Waves* as an image of the
personality, and with special reference to the relationship of outer
and inner. The image first appears in one of the impersonal
interludes; birds find a snail and tap "the shell against a stone. They
tapped furiously, methodically, until the shell broke and something
slimy oozed out from the crack" (p. 78). Later on Bernard uses
the same image. "A shell forms upon the soft soul," he says,
"nacreous, shiny, upon which sensations tap their beaks in vain"
(p. 181). Also see p. 88.

of a turbulent encroaching sea. The lighthouse is, of course, the central symbol of one of Virginia Woolf's most important novels, but she made far more extensive use of it than has generally been recognized. The image appears, in fact, in almost every book she wrote and is a key to an understanding of her work as a whole. It is important, moreover, to keep the total setting in mind—sea, as well as tower. Whatever the nature of the light source, whether it be a stark tower against the night sky, a lighted drawing-room window, a vast congeries of buildings, a searchlight, or even a glowworm flitting through dark caverns, the surrounding chaos is an integral part of the image. The lighthouse, in effect, is compounded of light and dark.

The image appears several times in Virginia Woolf's first novel. Whatever it may have come to mean, the lighthouse was related, as its origins show, to such trite figures of speech as "the light of civilization," "the torch of learning." In *The Voyage Out* the image has not yet been detached from these platitudes, and it may be that in the later novels remnants of this connection with universal ideas helped to strengthen Virginia Woolf's symbolism and prevented it from becoming too rarefied. The first hints of the image appear in the conversation of Richard and Clarissa Dalloway. It should be kept in mind that these Dalloways are not the relatively sophisticated pair of *Mrs. Dalloway*. In *The Voyage Out* they are portrayed as the worst sort of English Philistines: snobbish, terribly sure of their superiority, always spouting platitudes, and without an authentic idea in their heads. During one of their characteristic bouts of self-congratulation, Clarissa grows eloquent about the British Empire: "it makes one feel as if one couldn't bear *not* to be English!" she exclaims. "Think of the light burning over the House, Dick! When I stood on deck just now I seemed to see it. It's what one means by London" (p. 51). The juxtaposition of ideas is significant: the light burning over the House of Commons, London, and Clarissa gazing across the sea, imagining a glow in the distance. Her husband's reply reveals another aspect of the lighthouse image. " 'It's the continuity,' said Richard sententiously. A vision of English history, King following

King, Prime Minister Prime Minister, and Law Law had come over him while his wife spoke." The suggestion of rigid order and succession, the profusion of capital letters, the words "King," "Prime Minister," "Law," establish a connection between Clarissa's light burning over the House and the masculine principle.[33] The lighthouse is, of course, a masculine symbol, a great phallic tower, and this implication is retained in the later novels, where, not inappropriately, Virginia Woolf uses the image to suggest a union of the sexes. Another association of the lighthouse is suggested by another platitude, when Richard finds Helen Ambrose reading metaphysics. "It's the philosophers, it's the scholars," he rhapsodizes "they're the people who pass the torch, who keep the light burning by which we live" (p. 74). The lighthouse is associated with intellectual discipline, order, rationality. Dalloway's statement, trite as it is, contains an important truth to which even the Philistine pays lip service. Virginia Woolf's use of the lighthouse image was part of her endeavour to separate this truth, by which we live, from the mass of falsehoods with which it had become entangled.

The association of these and similar ideas with the lighthouse is amply borne out in other novels. In an early chapter of *Night and Day* Virginia Woolf describes the intellectual aristocracy, composed of a few distinguished families, to which Katharine Hilbery, granddaughter of the great poet Alardyce, belongs by right of birth. "They had been conspicuous judges and admirals, lawyers and servants of the State . . . and when they were not lighthouses firmly based on a rock for the guidance of their generation, they were steady, serviceable candles, illuminating the ordinary chambers of daily life" (p. 36). The metaphor appears again, developed more elaborately, in *Orlando*. The heroine, having lived into the eighteenth century and entered the highest society, happens to be present in a gathering of wits one night,

---

[33]   Cf. Virginia Woolf's comment, in *A Room of One's Own*, on "Mr. Kipling's officers who turn their backs; and his Sowers who sow the Seed; and his Men who are alone with their Work; and the Flag—one blushes at all these capital letters as if one had been caught eavesdropping at some purely masculine orgy" (p. 178).

when Mr. Pope walks in. Almost at once, by the light of his
genius, the tawdriness of the assembled company becomes
evident, and the poet destroys the last scraps of illusion by
making three bon mots, in comparison with which everything that has been said before appears stale and insipid. The
company are struck dumb; within twenty minutes they begin
to disperse. Such is the effect of "true wit, true wisdom, true
profundity." Orlando, however, finding herself next to the
poet on the stairs, invites him to come home with her. Sitting
together in her coach, they are obscured from each other by
long stretches of darkness and revealed to each other in brief
snatches of light as they pass lamp-posts along the way.
Orlando's attitude toward her companion undergoes corresponding alternations, becoming intensely critical during
the moments of light, but softening into something like
reverence whenever the darkness falls again. Finally, they
pass through a more brilliantly lighted area and are fully
exposed to each other. In the merciless glare, it seems to
Orlando that she and Pope are like "two wretched pigmies
on a stark desert land. . . . 'It is equally vain,' she thought, 'for
you to think you can protect me, or for me to think I can
worship you. . . . The light of truth is damnably unbecoming
to us both. " (pp. 206-7). A little further on Virginia Woolf
comments: "From the foregoing passage, however, it must
not be supposed that genius . . . is constantly alight, for then
we should see everything plain and perhaps should be
scorched to death in the process. Rather it resembles the lighthouse in its working, which sends one ray and then no more
for a time" (p. 207). The commonplace notion of the "light
of genius" is here being transformed into the more specific
image of the lighthouse, which is also somewhat closer to
being a viable metaphor. In *To the Lighthouse* a similar idea is
implied in Mr. Ramsay's despondent thoughts about the
limitations of his genius. "His own little light would shine,"
he broods, "not very brightly for a year or two, and would
then be merged in some bigger light, and that in a bigger still"
(p. 56). Perhaps more like a "serviceable candle" than a lighthouse, he is represented as fronting the night, standing "on
his little ledge facing the dark of human ignorance, how we

know nothing and the sea eats away the ground we stand on,"
yet maintaining a posture of admirable integrity, losing none
of his "intensity of mind" (pp. 68-69).[34]

The lighthouse is identified not only with great men in
history, but with the steady influence of institutions. The
universities, great twin pillars of the patriarchal society, cast
their radiance into the night and are seen in perspective
against the rough encircling sea. The image of Cambridge
as a kind of lighthouse appears in *Jacob's Room*. The context
is significant, for in this passage the classical scholar, Cowan,
representative of the masculine order, is placed in contrast
with Miss Umphelby who lectures at Newnham, it so
happens, on the same subject—Virgil. She "sings him
melodiously enough, accurately too, [but] she is always
brought up by this question . . . 'But if I met him, what should
I wear?'—and then . . . she lets her fancy play upon other
details of men's meeting with women. . . . Her lectures, therefore, are not half so well attended as those of Cowan, and the
thing she might have said in elucidation of the text for ever
left out" (p. 40). Her feminine approach, her impulse to translate even an academic discussion into personal terms, causes
her to be somewhat neglectful of strict scholarship. "In short,"
Virginia Woolf comments, "face a teacher with the image
of the taught and the mirror breaks." The breaking of the
mirror is perhaps to be interpreted as a mixed blessing: the
conventional frame of reference which stands between us
and reality has been destroyed, but without it one may at
times, like Miss Umphelby, find oneself at a loss. Virginia
Woolf now turns to the rival scholar whose lectures are so
well attended.

Cowan sipped his port, his exaltation over, no longer the
representative of Virgil. No, the builder, assessor, surveyor,
rather; ruling lines between names, hanging lists above doors.

[34] The lighthouse metaphor also appears in Virginia Woolf's essay
   on the *Memoirs* of Laetitia Pilkington, the midget who had
   known Swift. "Memories of great men are no infallible specific,"
   she wrote. "They fall upon the race of life like beams from a
   lighthouse. They flash, they shock, they reveal, they vanish." *The
   Common Reader* (1st ser.), p. 171.

Such is the fabric through which the light must shine, if shine
it can—the light of all these languages, Chinese and Russian,
Persian and Arabic, of symbols and figures, of history. . . . So
that if at night, far out at sea over the tumbling waves, one saw
a haze on the waters, a city illuminated, a whiteness even in the
sky, such as that now over the Hall of Trinity . . . that would
be the light burning there—the light of Cambridge" [p. 40].

The passage not only presents a vision of Cambridge as a
beacon over the sea, but it reminds us that the light is in
danger of being obscured. If Miss Umphelby's nemesis is
vagueness and inconsequence, Cowan's is loss of touch with
reality. He is in danger of turning into a mechanic, a mere
technician ruling lines. It may be that the true light requires
a "fabric," a masculine structure, to suspend it aloft, but it
must "shine through" and transcend the material.[35]

Masculine tower, feminine sea, a radiance somehow joining the two—the image of the lighthouse became, for Virginia Woolf, a symbol of the marriage of opposites, and, by
implication, of the androgynous mind. Reading a few key
passages, we can watch this happen. The best place to begin
is with Mrs. Ramsay's discovery of an impersonal reality,
the source of ineffable peace, which is in turn identified with
the lighthouse. Her experience is generalized, as yet, with
barely a hint that the luminous self is equivalent to the
androgynous mind. Mrs. Ramsay sits in the window, knitting
and thinking.

Not as oneself did one find rest ever, in her experience . . . but
as a wedge of darkness. Losing personality, one lost the fret, the
hurry, the stir; and there rose to her lips always some

[35]   Several other passages in the early novels link Cambridge, London,
and the lighthouse—e.g., *Jacob's Room*, pp. 29-30; *The Voyage Out*,
pp. 17-18. Cf. the passage in *Night and Day* where light from the
windows of the Hilbery drawing room, the light of "civilisation,"
is identified with the lighthouse. See p. 36, above. The three
lighted windows of the Hilbery drawing room may, perhaps, be
related to the three lighted windows at Jacob's college. "If any
light burns above Cambridge, it must be from three such rooms;
Greek burns here; science there; philosophy on the ground floor"
(*Jacob's Room*, p. 38). In *To the Lighthouse*, moreover, the beacon
sends out three strokes of light.

exclamation of triumph over life when things came together in this peace, this rest, this eternity; and pausing there she looked out to meet that stroke of the Lighthouse, the long steady stroke, the last of the three, which was her stroke, for watching them in this mood always at this hour one could not help attaching oneself to one thing especially of the things one saw; and this thing, the long steady stroke, was her stroke. Often she found herself sitting and looking . . . with her work in her hands until she became the thing she looked at—that light, for example [pp. 96-97].

The passage makes it clear that Mrs. Ramsay's ideal condition corresponds to the vision which Lily Briscoe has been seeking to capture in her painting. (Mrs. Ramsay aspires to be conscious of herself only "as a wedge of darkness," while Lily has been portraying her friend in oils as a "triangular purple shape" [p. 81].) It is interesting, moreover, that Mrs. Ramsay begins by thinking of the "wedge of darkness," and ends by identifying herself with the light; dark and light both seem to symbolize the same condition. Evidently Virginia Woolf has added a mystical element to the significance of the lighthouse as a cultural symbol. It is from the above passage that some critics derive the conclusion that the lighthouse stands for Mrs. Ramsay herself.[36] The statement is valid, as far as it goes, but surely more needs to be said about the lighthouse and the ideal condition which it symbolizes.

A passage dealing with the search for impersonal norms in *Night and Day* shows us Mrs. Ramsay's achievement in perspective. Ralph Denham aspires to the unity of being which Mrs. Ramsay embodies, and which is the source of her ineffable peace. He believes that he will be able to approach the ideal through his union with Katharine, that each will help the other to overcome his incompleteness. When Ralph feels

36 For example, Winifred Holtby, who writes: "in *To the Lighthouse* Mrs. Ramsay, alive or dead, gathers and concentrates all thought, all feeling, all action into herself. Her light reveals them. The long steady stroke which is her stroke illumines the island. She *is* the lighthouse, in some subtle way. The action, which in the first half of the book passes through her, is, in the second part, illuminated by her" (*Virginia Woolf*, p. 147).

himself in danger of losing Katharine, he tries to put this conviction into a letter.

He tried to convey to her the possibility that although human beings are woefully ill-adapted for communication, still, such communion is the best we know; moreover, they make it possible for each to have access to another world independent of personal affairs, a world of law, of philosophy, or more strangely a world such as he had had a glimpse of . . . when together they seemed to be sharing something, creating something, an ideal—a vision flung out in advance of our actual circumstances. If this golden rim were quenched, if life were no longer circled by an illusion (but was it an illusion after all?), then it would be too dismal an affair to carry to an end [p. 487].

Thus Virginia Woolf summed up what Ralph intended to say, but his letter was never finished; he became discouraged at the inadequacy of words, and especially when it came to conveying the mystical part of his vision. How could he explain what he meant by the "golden rim" that encircled life, and in some sense completed it? In desperation, he began doodling "blots fringed with flames meant to represent— perhaps the entire universe." He could not say himself precisely what they meant to him; they corresponded to his vision in some irrational way. A little later, reunited with Katharine, he lets her read the fragment of his letter on the scrap of paper, but she at once perceives that the most significant part of the message is contained in "the little dot with the flames around it."

Ralph nearly tore the page from her hand in shame and despair when he saw her actually contemplating the idiotic symbol of his most confused and emotional moments. . . .

It represented by its circumference of smudges surrounding a central blot all that encircling glow which for him surrounded, inexplicably, so many of the objects of life, softening their sharp outline, so that he could see certain streets, books, and situations wearing a halo almost perceptible to the physical eye. . . .

Quietly and steadily there rose up behind the whole aspect of life that soft edge of fire which gave its red tint to the atmosphere and crowded the scene with shadows [p. 493].

The blot, with its encircling glow, is another radiant source of light, closely related, if not exactly equivalent, to the lighthouse. It belongs to the same order of symbolism.[37] The lighthouse, as we have seen, symbolizes an ideal state of being, associated with Mrs. Ramsay. The blot fringed with flames performs a similar function for Ralph in the earlier novel. Furthermore, the blot is clearly a precursor of the dot with spokes radiating from it which Eleanor draws, or calls to mind, at several crucial moments in *The Years*. This later dot, a child's image of light, is associated with Eleanor's mystical liberation, her discovery of the core of the self; once again we are reminded of Mrs. Ramsay, "losing personality."[38] It seems that these three novels, *Night and Day*, *To the*

[37] The reddish glow may also be associated with the "light of love," as is suggested by a passage in *To the Lighthouse* where Lily Briscoe remembers the romance between Paul Rayley and Minta Doyle. "Suddenly . . . a reddish light seemed to burn in her mind, covering Paul Rayley, issuing from him. . . . For a sight, for a glory it surpassed everything in her experience, and burnt year after year like a signal fire on a desert island at the edge of the sea, and one had only to say 'in love' and instantly, as happened now, up rose Paul's fire again" (pp. 261–62). In *Night and Day* Katharine thinks of lovers as "the lantern bearers, whose lights, scattered among the crowd, wove a pattern" (p. 314).

[38] For Eleanor's experience, see pp. 100–103, above. There is another foreshadowing of Eleanor's dot in *Night and Day*. Mrs. Seal, one of Mary Datchet's co-workers in a feminist society, becomes very much involved in following an argument on the suffrage campaign. "One crucifix became entangled with another, and she dug a considerable hole in the table with the point of her pencil in order to emphasize the most striking heads of the discourse" (p. 265). A parallel scene in *The Years* shows us Eleanor, listening to the arguments at a suffrage meeting, drawing a dot with spokes radiating from it, and "prodding her pencil on the blotting paper" (p. 178). *To the Lighthouse* perhaps contains another variation on this theme in the scene where Lily Briscoe remembers sitting with Mrs. Ramsay on the beach, ramming a little hole in the sand, and covering it up, "by way of burying in it the perfection of the moment. It was like a drop of silver in which one dipped and illumined the darkness of the past" (p. 256). And in *Between the Acts* we are told that during Miss La Trobe's moments of "triumph, humiliation, ecstasy, despair . . . her heels had ground a hole in the grass" (p. 210).

Lighthouse, The Years, in many ways so different from each other, draw on a common source of inspiration, and even, to an extent, partake in a common symbolism.[39]

Ralph Denham's fire-fringed blot and impalpable glow, are somewhat vague equivalents for an abstruse ideal. But the lighthouse itself is explicitly referred to in *Night and Day*, in another context. The passage in which Ralph, wandering round London on a windy night, makes his way to Katharine's house and stands peering up at the three lighted windows of the Hilbery drawing room, likening them in his mind to a lighthouse, has been touched upon in an earlier chapter.[40] But the implications of the lighthouse image must be considered further. One of Ralph's resting places in the course of his wanderings is a bench on the Embankment, where he is approached by an old drunk, listens to snatches of a hard-luck story, and finally goes on his way, leaving the old man a "tribute of silver." Ralph has been wandering in search of someone to whom to communicate "something of the very greatest importance" (p. 393), something having to do with his love for Katharine, but his desire has been frustrated, the wind having blown great spaces between him and other people, just as it has blown away the old man's story. Ralph is angered by the old man's unwillingness to stop mumbling and listen to him. And "an odd image came to his mind of a lighthouse besieged by the flying bodies of lost

---

[39] Passages comparing the personality to a source of light occur in several other books—for example, *The Voyage Out*, where Hewet describes the self as a flaming wick. See pp. 108–9. The same metaphor also occurs in an often quoted passage in the essay on "Modern Fiction": "Examine for a moment an ordinary mind on an ordinary day. The mind receives a myriad impressions. . . . From all sides they come, an incessant shower of innumerable atoms; and as they fall, as they shape themselves into the life of Monday or Tuesday, the accent falls differently from of old. . . . Life is not a series of gig lamps symmetrically arranged; life is a luminous halo, a semi-transparent envelope surrounding us from the beginning of consciousness to the end." *The Common Reader* (1st ser.), p. 212. The self is directly compared to the "beam from a lighthouse" in *Orlando*, p. 312.

[40] See p. 36, above.

birds, who were dashed senseless, by the gales, against the glass. He had a strange sensation that he was both lighthouse and bird; he was steadfast and brilliant; and at the same time he was whirled, with all other things, senseless against the glass' (p. 394). At this crucial moment he is aware of opposing principles, of light, harmony, order, and of darkness, formlessness, within himself. With this image of the "lighthouse and the storm full of birds" still in his mind, guiding him, as it were, he turns his steps toward Katharine's house, which is indeed his beacon. Now, as he looks up at those windows, Ralph finds himself imagining that the source of the radiance issuing from them is Katharine herself. "He did not see her in the body; he seemed curiously to see her as a shape of light, the light itself; he seemed, simplified and exhausted as he was, to be like one of those lost birds fascinated by the lighthouse and held to the glass by the splendor of the blaze" (p. 395). A little while earlier Ralph had seen himself as both bird and lighthouse, but now his mood had changed. Katharine is his ideal, steadfast, whole, shining, and accordingly he sees himself as her opposite. But only for the moment. A little later Ralph encounters William Rodney, Katharine's rejected suitor, leaving her house, and again the image of the lighthouse is in his thoughts. This time it helps him to point the contrast between Katharine and himself on the one hand, and Rodney on the other. "He saw Rodney as one of the lost birds dashed senseless against the glass. . . . But he and Katharine were alone together, aloft, splendid, and luminous with a twofold radiance. He pitied the unstable creature beside him; he felt a desire to protect him, exposed without the knowledge which made his own way so direct" (p. 398). The metaphor represents, of course, the wholeness and fulfilment of requited love; it is in and through love, we need hardly add, that the opposites are united. With its image of Ralph and Katharine standing aloft in "twofold radiance," this passage seems unmistakably to be related to Virginia Woolf's description of the androgynous mind: "resonant . . . porous . . . [transmitting] emotion without impediment . . . incandescent . . . undivided."[41] When Denham

41   *A Room of One's Own*, p. 171.

and Rodney pause for a moment under a lamp-post (so Pope and Orlando confront each other), they have to "confess . . . the extreme depths of their folly," but, at the same time, "they seemed to be aware of some common knowledge which did away with the possibility of rivalry." Beams from the lighthouse cause all contentiousness to fade away.

A passage in *To the Lighthouse* strengthens the impression that the lighthouse image is related to the idea of androgyny. The final section of the novel, "The Lighthouse," has to do, in part, with tensions between Mr. Ramsay and his children, resentment generated by the father as the result of his one-sidedness. James's hatred is expressed by the image he associates with Mr. Ramsay of the scimitar "smiting through . . . leaves and flowers" (p. 276). James is remembering how his father shattered his hopes of going to the lighthouse many years earlier, when his mother was alive. There is an irony in the situation, for now that they have actually undertaken the voyage, positions are reversed; it is Mr. Ramsay who has almost to force his children to sail with him. New grievances still rankling in his mind, James thinks of the lighthouse as it seemed to him in the past and contrasts it with the lighthouse in front of him across the bay.

The Lighthouse was then [in the past] a silvery, misty-looking tower with a yellow eye, that opened suddenly, and softly in the evening. Now—

James looked at the Lighthouse. He could see the white-washed rocks; the tower, stark and straight; he could see that it was barred with black and white; he could see windows in it; he could even see washing spread on the rocks to dry. So that was the Lighthouse, was it?

No, the other was also the Lighthouse. For nothing was simply one thing. The other Lighthouse was true too [pp. 276–77].

The two lighthouses complement each other. The lighthouse of the present, the stark, straight tower "barred with black and white," is associated with Mr. Ramsay, and the masculine principle; the lighthouse of the past, the soft, "yellow eye that opened suddenly . . . in the evening," leads us back to the now dead Mrs. Ramsay, and the feminine principle. Looking across the bay, James begins to discover, perhaps for the first

time, that these lighthouses, of fact, and of memory, are re-
concilable, for nothing is "simply one thing." There must be
room in one's scheme of reality for the whole of experience.

The fact that Virginia Woolf associated the lighthouse
with a union of the sexes is borne out by her imagery in other
books. In *The Years* the lighthouse appears in the form of a
beam of light from a searchlight sweeping the sky during
World War I. Eleanor has been dining at her cousin Maggie's
house; during the evening there is a raid, an enemy plane
passes overhead, and when Eleanor comes out into the street
later, her thoughts of Maggie and her husband Renny blend
with the sight of the moving beacon across the night sky.
"That is the man . . . that I should like to have married," she
realizes suddenly, saying goodnight to Renny. Then her
thoughts pass on beyond herself.

And a scene came before her; Maggie and Renny sitting over the
fire. A happy marriage, she thought, that's what I was feeling all
the time. A happy marriage. She looked up as she walked down
the dark little street. . . . A broad fan of light, like the sail of a
windmill, was sweeping slowly across the sky. It seemed to take
what she was feeling and to express it broadly and simply, as if
another voice were speaking in another language. Then the light
stopped and examined a fleecy patch of sky, a suspected spot.
The raid! she said to herself. I'd forgotten the raid! . . . She
was surprised but it was true [pp. 299-300].

Similarly, in Virginia Woolf's late story, "The Searchlight,"
fans of light wheel across the sky while a lady sitting on a
balcony after dinner with her friends reminisces about the
union of her grandfather and grandmother. She conjures up
a picture for her listeners of her grandfather, alone in his
ancestral tower, surrounded by vast expanses of moor and
sky and surveying the world through a telescope. Slowly, he
brings more and more details of the earth into focus, until
finally the powerful lenses pick out a remote cottage among
trees, and show him a man and woman kissing. "It was the
first time he had seen a man kiss a woman—" the lady comments, "in his telescope—miles and miles away across the
moors!"[42] The vision inspires him to descend from his tower

42   In *A Haunted House*, pp. 119-20.

and to seek out his future wife, who became the lady's grandmother. Then the lens of the telescope, the frame in which the symbolic couple had appeared in each other's arms, is linked with the searchlight beams that have been playing in the sky while the story was told. "A shaft of light fell upon Mrs. Ivimey [the narrator] as if someone had focussed the lens of a telescope upon her." Those powerful rays, extending not only through space, but across the years, present a symbol of union akin to the vision of man and woman against the sky in *Between the Acts* and *The Years*, and link the lighthouse image to the theme of mystical marriage.[43] It is perhaps the fact that Virginia Woolf used the image to suggest this union that accounts for the variety of interpretations advanced by critics. James Hafley, prefacing an excellent summary of comments on the lighthouse in *The Glass Roof*, writes: "Almost every critic explains the lighthouse differently—and almost every critic makes what would seem to be the mistake of finding the lighthouse simply one thing" (p. 79). Like the idea of the androgynous mind, the lighthouse combines opposing principles; it is both phallus and eye, at times, erect and stark, at others, misty, yielding.

Making allowance for the far greater scope of the novel, the lighthouse image plays a part in *To the Lighthouse* analogous to that of the snail in "The Mark on the Wall." Both are symbols of resolution to which the mind turns when the stress of conflict has become very great; both have a twofold nature and thus express the union of opposites. Both symbolize a state of transcendence, as David Daiches observes of the lighthouse in a perceptive comment.

The lighthouse itself, standing lonely in the midst of the sea, is a symbol of the individual who is at once a unique being and a part of the flux of history. To reach the lighthouse is, in a sense, to make contact with a truth outside oneself, to surrender the uniqueness of one's ego to an impersonal reality. Mr. Ramsay, who is an egotist constantly seeking applause and

---

[43]   The image of the searchlight appears, briefly, at the beginning of *The Years*. "Slowly wheeling, like the rays of a searchlight, the days, the weeks, the years passed one after another across the sky" (p. 4).

encouragement from others, resents his young son's enthusiasm
for visiting the lighthouse, and only years later, when his wife
has died and his own life is almost worn out, does he win this
freedom from self—and it is significant that Virginia Woolf
makes Mr. Ramsay escape his egotistic preoccupations for the
first time just before the boat finally reaches the lighthouse.
Indeed, the personal grudges nourished by each of the
characters fall away just as they arrive.[44]

This statement seems consonant with the interpretation of
the lighthouse presented here, provided one adds that, to
Virginia Woolf, "freedom from self" implied the attaining
of the androgynous mind, and that the ego which her novel
teaches us to shun is closely bound up with imbalance, masculine one-sidedness. That the conflict is drawn along sexual
lines is borne out in the last section of *To the Lighthouse*, where
the role of the lighthouse as mediator and symbol of resolution becomes increasingly clear.

The antagonism between Mr. Ramsay and his children
stems, essentially, from the same differences as the dispute
about the weather between husband and wife in the first part
of the novel. James and Cam, in their minds, accuse their
father of being tyrannical and one-sided, of disregarding
their feelings, though displaying, as ever, a remarkable grasp
of facts which puts them at a disadvantage in contending
with him. James, in particular, carries on the debate in behalf
of his dead mother, or, perhaps more accurately, invokes his
mother's influence in order to free himself from the domina-
tion of his father. The lighthouse toward which James and
Mr. Ramsay are sailing represents different values for each of
them. Mr. Ramsay is achieving freedom from self, performing the difficult task of renunciation, while his son is at the
stage of finding himself for the first time, of proving his manhood. The lighthouse, however, remains a symbol of wholeness; James gains what he is lacking; Mr. Ramsay renounces
traits that he has carried to excess. Both of them have matured
as a result of the voyage, though in different ways; and by
this process of addition and subtraction they have become
more nearly equals. A reconciliation between father and son

[44]   *Virgina Woolf*, p. 86.

is now possible. Let us consider the events leading up to this reconciliation.

Although the voyage derives from Mr. Ramsay's impulse to do something in memory of his wife ("rites he went through for his own pleasure in memory of dead people" [p. 246]), the quiet opposition of his children, perpetuating Mrs. Ramsay's influence, her side in the dialogue, is still necessary to keep them all on course toward the lighthouse. It is James who does the steering, a fact which is not merely incidental, as Cam perceives: "his hand on the tiller had become symbolical to her" (p. 251). Keeping his eye fixed on the lighthouse, James denounces his father in his mind. His words make one think of Virginia Woolf's own denunciations of the patriarchy. "Whatever he did [James resolved] . . . he would fight . . . he would track down and stamp out —tyranny, despotism, he called it—making people do what they did not want to do, cutting off their right to speak" (p. 274). (Cam, for her part, remembers waking in the night, "trembling with rage," because of some command of her father's, "some insolence: 'Do this,' 'Do that,' his dominance: his 'Submit to me' " [p. 253].) James's belief in himself, and his determination to resist, are increased by a sight of the beacon tower: "he might do anything, he felt, looking at the Lighthouse and the distant shore" (p. 274). And all the while, his mind keeps harking back to a scene in his childhood, when his father had interrupted, with a demand for sympathy, while Mrs. Ramsay was reading to James from a book of fairy tales, and had "disturbed the perfect simplicity and good sense of his relations with his mother" (p. 58). James's resentment is compounded of jealousy and of anger at the injury which he senses being done to his mother. For in order to solace her husband, Mrs. Ramsay must transform herself into a fountain of sympathy; the effort required is both physically exhausting and spiritually degrading. "There tinged her physical fatigue some faintly disagreeable sensation with another origin. . . . She did not like, even for a second, to feel finer than her husband; and further, could not bear not being entirely sure, when she spoke to him, of the truth of what she said" (p. 61). As James looks toward the lighthouse, he realizes what the quality was in his mother that he so highly prizes. "She alone spoke the truth; to her alone could he speak it. That was the source of her everlasting attraction for him, perhaps; she was a person to whom one could say what came into one's head. But all the time he thought of her, he was conscious of his father following his thought, surveying it, making it shiver and falter" (p. 278). Under the spell of this conflict, paralyzed by his memories, and powerless to flick off "the grains of misery," James sits "with his hand on the tiller," staring toward the symbolic lighthouse.

At the same time, Lily Briscoe, her easel set up on shore, a view of the bay before her, is also aware of the conflict; she too, in her way, has been trying to work it out, to find a resolution. In her thoughts the opposing forces are named more explicitly, perhaps, than elsewhere. The Ramsays' efforts to reach the lighthouse have been paralleled by Lily's struggles to finish her painting. As James's mind is clouded by thoughts of his father's tyranny, Lily's vision of her picture is disturbed by some disproportion in the scene before her, as if disharmony in the distant ship had become visible to her eyes. She realizes that she has not been successful in transferring her elusive vision onto canvas. "She had been wasting her morning. For whatever reason she could not achieve that razor edge of balance between two opposite forces; Mr. Ramsay and the picture" (p. 287).⁴⁵ And Lily's picture, we

---

⁴⁵ It is interesting to compare this with Lily's statement earlier in the novel of her problem with the picture: "It was a question . . . how to connect this mass on the right hand with that on the left. She might do it by bringing the line of the branch across so; or break the vacancy in the foreground by an object (James perhaps) so. But the danger was that by doing that the unity of the whole might be broken" (pp. 82–83). Her thought of using James to make the connection is suggestive, in view of his role now at the tiller. Her aim, as she expresses it later on, is to create something "beautiful and bright . . . on the surface, feathery and evanescent, one colour melting into another like the colours on a butterfly's wing; but beneath the fabric must be clamped together with bolts of iron" (p. 255). At the very end of the novel Lily moves the position of the tree (tree equals lighthouse?) as she had intended earlier—"she drew a line there, in the centre"—and solves the problem of connecting the masses.

recall, is equivalent to Mrs. Ramsay's ordering of experience —in a sense, to Mrs. Ramsay herself. Lily's problem, like James's, may be expressed in terms of her need to cope with the disturbing influence of Mr. Ramsay (masculine onesidedness). Both of them can do so only through the mediation of Mrs. Ramsay (wholeness, the androgynous mind). A little later, as Lily's thoughts revolve upon family life, she associates the Ramsays' marriage with a scene in her mind of Mrs. Ramsay as a girl being handed on shore from a boat by the man who was to become her husband. "Letting herself be helped by him, Mrs. Ramsay had thought (Lily supposed) the time has come now. Yes, she would say it now. Yes, she would marry him. And she stepped slowly, quietly on shore" (p. 295).[46] That landing is soon to be symbolically re-enacted by Mr. Ramsay at the lighthouse. With his arrival there the union of the Ramsays is, as it were, consummated, the husband becoming reconciled at last with the spirit of his dead wife.

That event is heralded, as David Daiches has observed, by the falling away of grudges. On the verge of landing, James watches his father, "getting his head now against the Lighthouse, now against the waste of waters," (the conflicting elements in precarious balance) and begins to regard him sympathetically, identifying Mr. Ramsay with "that loneliness which was for both of them the truth about things" (p. 301). The lighthouse looms above James in the guise of masculine symbol: "a stark tower on a bare rock. It satisfied him. It confirmed some obscure feeling of his about his own character." At once, as if to emphasize his new-found manhood, the opposing force comes in. "The old ladies, he thought, thinking of the garden at home, went dragging

---

46 Cf. Mrs. Hilbery's account to Katharine in *Night and Day* of her betrothal: "We were in a little boat going out to a ship at night. . . . The sun had set and the moon was rising over our heads. There were lovely silver lights upon the waves and three green lights upon the steamer in the middle of the bay. Your father's head looked so grand against the mast. It was life, it was death. The great sea was round us. It was the voyage for ever and ever" (p. 483).

their chairs about on the lawn. Old Mrs. Beckwith, for example, was always saying how nice it was . . . and how they
ought to be so proud . . . but as a matter of fact, James thought,
looking at the Lighthouse stood there on its rock, it's like
that. He looked at his father. . . . They shared that knowledge" (pp. 301-2). For James, the culmination of the voyage
comes when his father turns and praises his steering. This is
what he has been waiting for, as his sister is aware. "There!
Cam thought, addressing herself silently to James. You've
got it at last. . . . He was so pleased that he would not look at
her or at his father or at any one" (p. 306). The gift that Mr.
Ramsay has given his son is the freedom to be himself.[47]
Now the scene has been set for the symbolic renewal of the
father that brings the novel to a close. In Lily Briscoe's mind,
concentrating on the voyage from the distance, Mr. Ramsay
and the lighthouse seem to merge as she imagines him landing
there. "The Lighthouse had become almost invisible, had
melted away into a blue haze, and the effort of looking at
it and the effort of thinking of him landing there . . . both
seemed to be one and the same effort" (p. 308). Lily also has
played her part in his transformation. "Whatever she had
wanted to give him, when he left her that morning, she had
given him at last." And she intones words that link this event
with the great archetype of death and rebirth: "He has
landed. . . . It is finished."

From close by, as witnessed by Cam and James, the landing
is real enough. But Mr. Ramsay has changed. He is strikingly
youthful, stepping before them toward the goal, transformed, so that in his bearing he seems to embody newfound
freedom, as if he were rejecting the masculine deity, and
casting off his one-sidedness forever. "He rose and stood in

[47] Jean Sudrann observes that Cam's experience parallels her brother's
"symbolic journey to maturity. . . . As James becomes adult and
male on this journey, so Cam comes into a female heritage. It is
no accident that throughout the sail James's attention is directed
toward the Lighthouse and Cam's toward the sea and the island,
nor that it is Cam who feels the 'fountain of joy' in the sea."
"The Sea, the City and the Clock: A Study of Symbolic Form in
the Novels of Virginia Woolf" (Ph.D. dissertation, Columbia,
1950).

the bow of the boat, very straight and tall, for all the world, James thought, as if he were saying, 'There is no God,' and Cam thought, as if he were leaping into space, and they both rose to follow him as he sprang, lightly like a young man, holding his parcel, on to the rock."

·✦{ 5 }✦·

Feminism and Art

I

Mr. Ramsay's landing on the rock is a symbol of illumination; it stands for a unity of being that can be attained only now and then by the rare individual wrestling with his soul. It is an experience that takes place in solitude, and, as the crucial moment of *To the Lighthouse* approaches, we are reminded of Mr. Ramsay's essential loneliness, in spite of the shadowy presence of his children. It is a mystery and transcends the temporal order; the solitary old man seems to be "leaping into space." In the lighthouse Virginia Woolf found a symbol that perfectly conveyed her meaning. But she succeeded only by excluding areas of experience that were extremely important to her. In order to create the context in which the lighthouse could function as a symbol she had to maintain the action of the novel at some level above, or beyond, that of concrete reality. Its pages are full of scenes that seem almost to have a consciousness of their own; of objects that quiver on the verge of dissolving into metaphors. In her last novels, on the other hand, Virginia Woolf turned her attention to capturing the poetry of solid objects and practical life. In the nineteen-thirties she was becoming "more and more interested in politics, more and more aware of the threat of another war, more and more concerned to understand simple people and to grasp underlying fundamental forces."[1] This growing interest in practical affairs did not, however, cause her to give up trying to express visionary experience; it made her resolve, rather, to be both mystical and practical at once. A comparison of *To the Lighthouse* and *The Years* shows the lines along which she was developing. In the later novel she relinquished the use of a dramatic central symbol. Eleanor's vision, though related to Mrs. Ramsay's unity of being, is hinted at and only half-expressed. For the sake of conveying to her readers the absolute reality of the scenes and objects she was describing, Virginia Woolf diffused her symbolism throughout the book, softened its effect, broke the lighthouse into fragments, as it were. Rather than leading to a weakening of her characteristic qualities, this change resulted in a deepening of her vision. *The Years* is greater in scope, and more consistent in tone, than *To the Lighthouse*. The linear simplicity of its plot is more suggestive than the stylized design of the earlier book. Visionary elements no longer stand boldly outlined against the sky but are integrated with other events, joining in the broad stream of life. They accost the reader amid familiar surroundings and insinuate themselves into his mind by their naturalness. Solid objects like the spotted walrus, scenes like that of the dawning day, hint a transcendent meaning without making the reader aware that they are being manipulated for his benefit.

There is a corresponding change in Virginia Woolf's handling of social themes. They are more fully integrated. Feminism no longer obtrudes, as it did occasionally even in *To the Lighthouse*. *The Years* is permeated with social consciousness, but its tone is objective. The feminist point of view, which is an essential part of both novels, has become dispassionate in the later work. *To the Lighthouse* is based on

---

[1]   Aileen Pippett, *The Moth and the Star: A Biography of Virginia Woolf* (Boston, 1955), p. 298.

the premise that only the eternal feminine can keep men on course toward spiritual illumination. *The Years* develops a similar theme in terms that are both more particular and more universal. Radiance transforms Eleanor's old age because she has learned sympathetically to unite masculine and feminine sides of her mind. *To the Lighthouse* can be read as an attack on the male sex; *The Years* cannot.

As a novelist, Virginia Woolf labored to join fact and vision, to shape "globed compacted things" in accordance with her artistic ideals. But as a controversialist her aims were less clear. She tried, not altogether wholeheartedly, to produce pure social criticism. *Three Guineas* was to be her definitive statement about the practical side of reality, a kind of feminist manifesto. It was to be more concerned with doctrine, less modified by fantasy, than *A Room of One's Own*. The time had come, Virginia Woolf felt, to launch an all-out attack against the patriarchy. But she was not really cut out for writing manifestos. In spite of the genuineness of her indignation, *Three Guineas* is a rather pallid book. There is an unresolved contradiction in it. While Virginia Woolf the controversialist is battling for certain reforms, the insidious voice of Virginia Woolf the artist keeps chiming in, implying that there is a higher reality, a realm which practical politics cannot enter. The tone of her argument is subtly wrong. Occasional hints, not only of satire, but of levity, undermine its seriousness. The ways of the world, especially the masculine official world, always seemed ludicrous to Virginia Woolf. One is reminded of Beatrice Webb's condescending remark about her husband's cabinet post, "My little boy shall have his toys," which Mrs. Woolf noted approvingly in her diary.[2] In *Three Guineas* she was trying to play the politics game herself, and at the same time to remain detached, to be both part of the battle and above it.

One important aspect of the book reveals this contradiction very clearly. In addition to attacking the patriarchy, Virginia Woolf presents a feminist program, a plan of action for women. Her proposals combine the calculated rage of

[2]   *A Writer's Diary*, October 23, 1929, p. 145.

the demagogue with the spirituality of the saint. She seems, at one moment, to be inclined toward pure anarchy, and the next, to favor a monastic rule. Here, as elsewhere, she is striving to reconcile opposites, but the very nature of *Three Guineas* as a feminist tract prevents her from succeeding. It is one thing to describe an ideal state of harmony, as she did in *The Years*, and something else to describe policies that will discourage nations from going to war. Virginia Woolf's attempt to translate her vision of peace from the realm of art to that of politics was quixotic. Although its avowed purpose was to further the peace movement, *Three Guineas* may well have had a contrary effect. Q. D. Leavis, in a scathing review, claimed that Virginia Woolf's emphasis upon her class, sex, and even profession, was an incitement to snobbery.[3] It is true that *Three Guineas* was marred by an attitude very like the aggressiveness that Virginia Woolf deplored in men. This fault may be attributed, no doubt, to the anguish of "a sensitive woman who passionately desires peace and is almost in despair in a world rushing towards war."[4] It suggests, however, that her social criticism tended to lose its meaning when removed from the imaginative contexts of her fiction. The feminist in her needed the support of the artist.

This conclusion can be tested by looking more closely at *Three Guineas* and *The Years*. These volumes, it should be remembered, were so much identified in Virginia Woolf's mind that she could lump them together as "one book."[5]

3   "Caterpillars of the Commonwealth, Unite," *Scrutiny*, 7 (September, 1938): 209. Mrs. Leavis warned her readers "that Mrs. Woolf thinks this class—the relatively very few wealthy propertied people in our country—is to be identified with 'the educated class' and contains at this date the average educated man and the average student of the women's colleges of the older universities. This is the first of many staggering intimations for the reader that Mrs. Woolf is not living in the contemporary world; almost the first thing we notice is that the author of *Three Guineas* is quite insulated by class." Deeply piqued, Q. D. Leavis concluded that the daughter of Leslie Stephen was in reality an insider masquerading in outsider's clothing.
4   Pippett, *The Moth and the Star*, p. 303.
5   *A Writer's Diary*, June 3, 1938, p. 284.

Both reveal the same highmindedness, the same fierce struggle to reconcile practical and artistic goals. But there the similarity ends. The novel is a *tour de force* of objectivity; the tract is an exercise in special pleading. The feminist program which forms the heart of *Three Guineas* exposes Virginia Woolf's limitations as surely as the luminous narrative of *The Years* proves her mastery. Taken together, these two books encompass the best and the worst of which she was capable. By describing their discords and harmonies we describe the balance of forces upon which her artistic success depended.

Before discussing Virginia Woolf's feminist program we must ask, To whom was she speaking? She explicitly defined her audience in *Three Guineas*. So many daughters of educated men, she said, were dependent on the patriarchy for their living that it would be unrealistic to appeal to them as a class. If she were going to ask women to help prevent war by protecting culture and intellectual liberty, she would have to narrow her target down to those among them who possessed an independent income. So to her salutation, "Daughters of educated men," she added, "who have enough to live upon." But once again she hesitated. Could she assume that there really existed "1000, 500 or even 250" women who had been able, by her exacting standards, to preserve their intellectual purity? Having considered the possibility that there might, indeed, be no one to hear it, she went on finally to make her appeal. Even if this is a rhetorical flourish, it reveals a curious attitude on the part of the writer. In her own imagination, the circle of readers or disciples is constantly narrowing. Her message is not for women in general, or even for women of her own class, but for a hard core of the financially and morally independent. In apparently renouncing any thought of appealing to a wider audience she may have been acting like a serious artist, but not like a serious reformer. Her program, like her art, was intended to inspire a tiny elite—the group to whom she increasingly referred as "outsiders."[6]

Certain other attitudes implicit in *Three Guineas* should be kept in mind. The most important of these is that women are morally superior to men, an idea which was also suggested in her novels. Ironically enough, the one advantage that goes along with being considered inferior is that one escapes the corruption of power. Women have benefited to the full from this advantage. Having been used to ridicule all their lives, they are less afraid than men to incur ridicule in support of good causes. Having been denied preferment, they have no sinecures to lose. Having been excluded by the Church and the universities, they have had little to do with the prostitution of religion or learning. They have been preserved by countless humiliations from the "great modern sins of vanity, egotism, and megalomania" (p. 149). In the arts, too, they have a potential advantage, since creative objectivity comes more naturally to them than to men who are embroiled in competition. Virginia Woolf goes so far as to call the poverty of women a veritable blessing: "The law of England sees to it that we do not inherit great possessions," she exclaims; "the law of England denies us, and let us hope will long continue to deny us, the full stigma of nationality" (p. 149). Hence women are more receptive than men to idealistic and humanitarian appeals, such as the one she is addressing to them. "It should not be difficult," she suggests, "to transmute the old ideal of bodily chastity into the new ideal of mental chastity—to hold that if it was wrong to sell the body for money it is much more wrong to sell the mind for money" (p. 150). Women thus form a kind of human reservoir into which virtues neglected by society have fallen.

---

6   While not all daughters of educated men should necessarily be considered outsiders, those in the ranks of the outsiders, Virginia Woolf implies, will be recruited exclusively from among the daughters of educated men. The Outsiders' Society, she says at one point, "would consist of educated men's daughters working in their own class—how indeed can they work in any other?—and by their own methods for liberty, equality and peace" (*Three Guineas*, p. 193).

These virtues are innate, not merely acquired, though the part that character plays in proportion to circumstance is impossible to determine.[7] Society and the arts can be rejuvenated only by restoring the despised feminine elements to their proper place among the faculties of man. It follows that women, as the chief bearers of the feminine qualities, have a mission to bring about this regeneration, a mission for which their long martyrdom has made them especially fit.

Three Guineas was intended to help women fulfil this destiny by stating guidelines for action. Virginia Woolf had repeatedly pointed out that women could do no good by imitating the ways of men, no matter how successfully. In *Three Guineas* she tried to suggest an alternative. She wished to describe a way of life that would be truly in accord with the female psyche, to promulgate a Law of Moses for the outsider. Her task was complicated by the fact that anything like a code or system was, by her definition, unfeminine. She was determined, nevertheless, to give her readers some specific advice. Even a few women, she believed, living truly to themselves, would exert a great force for good in the world. But while she stressed the practical significance of her proposals, she was also forced to admit that many of them would never be realized in this world.

The first problem the social reformer should attack, according to Virginia Woolf, is the problem of education. Her program in education arises from a kind of dialectic between

7   This is the view, I believe, that emerges from a reading of *Three Guineas* as a whole, though one passage seems to contradict it. Observing that the way of virtue is easier for women than for their brothers, Virginia Woolf wrote: "They are immune, through no merit of their own, from certain compulsions. To protect culture and intellectual liberty in practice would mean, as we have said, ridicule and chastity, loss of publicity and poverty. But those, as we have seen, are their familiar teachers." The bitter words "through no merit of their own" were meant to call attention to the degree to which women have been helpless to alter their condition. She seems to have had no doubt, however, that women are innately free of certain vices that are common in men, e.g., the need for violence. See the section on the evils of the patriarchy, pp. 82–91, above.

existing institutions and an ideal college for which she
sketched her plan in *Three Guineas*. The ideal college is the
very opposite of an "institution." It is fluid, "experimental,"
"adventurous." Its boundaries are forever shifting; it is built
"of some cheap, easily combustible material which does not
hoard dust and perpetuate traditions" (p. 61). It is a place—
or more accurately, perhaps, a sphere of influence—within
which nothing dead is to be perpetuated—neither dead
religion ("Do not have chapels") nor dead art and erudition
("Do not have museums and libraries with chained books
and first editions under glass cases"). The curriculum is to be
composed with particular concern for the preservation of
life and freedom. "The arts of dominating . . . of ruling, of
killing, of acquiring land and capital" are to be strictly
ignored. The liberal, life-preserving arts, "medicine, mathematics, music, painting and literature," will form the curriculum, along with the unrecognized domestic arts "of
human intercourse; the art of understanding other people's
lives and minds, and the little arts of talk, of dress, of cookery"
(p. 62).[8] It is to be a college that offers few lectures, sets no
examinations, confers no degrees, a place to which teachers
will gladly come because they will be free to learn there. The
chief safeguard of its integrity is to be poverty, for this will
insure the absence of competition. In token of this fact,
Virginia Woolf named her imaginary college "the poor
college." It might have been more accurate to call it "the
anti-college," for her thinking on the subject was mainly
negative and scarcely applicable to real problems, as she herself was aware. She had started inventing the poor college
while trying to make up her mind whether or not to make a
contribution to a real, and struggling, women's college. She
had been asking herself what conditions she could impose
upon the recipients of her gift. Suddenly, her fantasy was
interrupted by quite a different vision: she seemed to see the
treasurer of the real women's college reminding her, almost

---

8   One effect of such a curriculum might well be to "bring out and
fortify the differences" between the sexes, a result which Virginia
Woolf had favored in *A Room of One's Own*, pp. 152–53.

piteously, that the graduates must earn their livings, that employers prefer applicants with letters after their names, and that degrees, lectures, examinations, are indispensable. The women's college must continue to imitate the older patriarchal institutions, or cease to exist. Virginia Woolf's contribution must therefore be sent with no conditions attached to it, in spite of her ambivalence.

Here, as so often happens in *Three Guineas*, Virginia Woolf has built an imaginary edifice, only to demolish it a moment later. Her conflicting aims tend to cancel each other out. Having done with the "poor college," she turns to more practical proposals. Outsiders should work individually for educational reform, she says. They should "refuse to teach any art or science that encourages war"—in other words, strictly limit their professional careers (p. 67). They should boycott those "cities of strife," the two leading universities, and refuse to accept their degrees or "to take office or honour" from them (p. 204). They should exert a constant pressure of tacit ridicule against prizes, distinctions, ranks, examinations.[9]

This attack upon current modes of education is typical of Virginia Woolf's reactions to patriarchal customs and institutions. In effect, she counseled outsiders to remain outside, and by keeping their distance to retain the advantage that distance confers. Aided by their detachment, they were to become relentless critics, gadflies to the state. Disinterestedness is the proudest ornament that women can boast, Virginia Woolf reminded them, and must be preserved at all costs. She warned them not to take any part in patriarchal rites. They were to avoid not only societies but official pageants,

---

9   Rachel and Terence's ideas on the education of their children, in *The Voyage Out*, whimsically foreshadow these proposals. They sketch "an outline of the ideal education—how their daughter should be required from infancy to gaze at a large square of cardboard, painted blue, to suggest thoughts of infinity, for women were grown too practical; and their son—he should be taught to laugh at great men, that is, at distinguished successful men, at men who wore ribands and rose to the tops of their trees" (pp. 294–95).

coronations, state funerals, and the like. Outsiders should refuse to wear the special uniforms that are designed for these functions; they should swear no oaths; above all, they should refuse to accept official or semi-official distinctions of the kind that are advertised by "medals, honours, degrees . . . all tokens that culture has been prostituted and intellectual liberty sold into captivity" (p. 271).[10]

She herself had begun refusing honors long before she wrote *Three Guineas*. In 1927, in a letter to Victoria Sackville-West, she told of having been asked "to give the *Femina Vie Heureuse* prize to a Frenchman." When the woman representing the committee, a Lady Dilke, refused to take "no" for an answer, she frightened her off by pleading that she had no clothes to wear, a ruse that worked immediately. "Also, I think I've got out of lunching with her on the same plea," she went on. "It's true too. Never shall I buy another skirt. Never shall I give a prize to a Frenchman. And, by the way . . . she said something about giving *me* the prize, and I blushed all over, holding the telephone, with shame and ignominy. This is true. Snobbish? No: instinctive; right."[11] A few years later, ironically just at a time when she was writing a denunciation of society in *The Years*, a letter from the University of Manchester announced that they wished to confer an honorary degree of Doctor of Letters upon her. "Nothing would induce me to connive at all that humbug," she noted in her diary.[12] In 1935 she tersely alluded to another refusal of a higher honor. "The Prime Minister's letter offering to recommend me for the Companion of Honour. No."[13] She did not consider these refusals as sacrifices, since the prospect of receiving honors and awards gave her no pleasure.

From their vantage point "outside society," Virginia Woolf proposed in *Three Guineas*, women would undertake to "investigate the claims of all public societies to which . . .

10 For other passages supporting these general principles, see *Three Guineas*, pp. 146, 193, 206-7.
11 Quoted by Pippett, *The Moth and the Star*, p. 248.
12 *A Writer's Diary*, March 25, 1933, pp. 189-90.
13 *Ibid.*, May 13, 1935, p. 240.

they are forced to contribute as taxpayers as carefully and fearlessly as they would investigate the claims of private societies to which they contribute voluntarily" (p. 204). Like the universities, the Church would be carefully scrutinized. Outsiders would look into the writings of "divines and historians"; they would consider the current conception of God (which, according to Virginia Woolf, is decidedly "of patriarchal origin"). They would not hesitate to propose radical innovations in religion. "By criticizing religion they would attempt to free the religious spirit from its present servitude and would help, if need be, to create a new religion," more in accord with the real intentions of the founder of Christianity (p. 205).[14]

In the professions, outsiders could exert an influence far out of proportion to their numbers. Virginia Woolf advised that they should "bind themselves to earn their own livings," thereby securing the only real guarantee of their independence (p. 200). The right to work freed women to fight for their ideals; it must be considered a weapon in the struggle against war, and jealously guarded. Outsiders should agitate, together with other groups, for a living wage in all professions open to them, and for the creation of new opportunities. But beyond this point, they would part company with the organized reformers. For one thing, they would resolutely oppose many current practices that turn the professions into battlefields. They would struggle against exclusiveness. Every profession should be open to any human being who is able to qualify for it, be he "man or woman, black or white" (p. 121). Furthermore, the best safeguard of integrity in the professions, as in the ideal college, is poverty. Virginia Woolf proposed, therefore, that outsiders pledge themselves to earn just enough to buy "that modicum of health, leisure, knowledge . . . that is needed for the full

[14]   In protesting against the exclusion of women from the priesthood, Virginia Woolf observed "that the founder of Christianity believed that neither training nor sex was needed for this profession." There was no justification for excluding women, she said, "since they were thought fit by the founder of the religion and by one of his apostles to preach" (pp. 221, 222).

development of body and mind. But no more. Not a penny more" (p. 145).[15] As far as possible they should refuse to sell the products of their brains for money, giving their services without a fee once they had satisfied their material needs. As we can see, Virginia Woolf was using the term "poverty" loosely. Outsiders might enjoy all the comforts they were accustomed to without infringing her rule. By virtue of their disinterestedness, these women practicing their professions "experimentally, in the interests of research and for love of the work itself," would come to occupy key positions and would be able to play the role of public tribunes. "They would bind themselves to obtain full knowledge of professional practices, and to reveal any instance of tyranny or abuse" (p. 204). They would form, in effect, an austere guild within the professions, and, at the same time, above them.

For understandable reasons, Virginia Woolf placed special emphasis, in her program, on the profession of literature. Women who practice this profession, she wrote, are in a favored position. Unlike their fellow outsiders, they have a tradition behind them, and they have found a measure of acceptance in their field. "The profession of literature," she reminded her readers, ". . . is the only profession which did not fight a series of battles in the nineteenth century" over the admission of women (p. 162). Outsiders must pledge themselves "not to commit adultery of the brain," and by "adultery of the brain" is meant, to write "what you do not want to write for the sake of money" (pp. 169, 170). This brain adultery is worse than adultery of the body, because bad books and articles tend to propagate the vices which bred them, whereas those who sell their bodies take "good care that the matter shall end there." The proposals of publishers, editors, lecture agents, who deal in "the brain

15   Cf. her comment in *A Room of One's Own* on the piling up of excess wealth: "Watch in the spring sunshine the stockbroker and the great barrister going indoors to make money and more money and more money when it is a fact that five hundred pounds a year will keep one alive in the sunshine. These are unpleasant instincts to harbour, I reflected. They are bred of the conditions of life; of the lack of civilization" (p. 66).

selling trade," should be resented and exposed with as much indignation as would be the proposals of other "pimps and Panders." The prohibition against brain adultery applied not only to writing for money but to all forms of "advertisement and publicity." Virginia Woolf admonished the outsider "not to appear on public platforms . . . not to allow [her] private face to be published, or details of [her] private life" (pp. 170-71). Furthermore, she should refuse to subscribe to "papers that encourage intellectual slavery" and should stay away from "lectures that prostitute culture" (p. 179).

At this point, Virginia Woolf supposed her listener objecting that it was too much to ask her to give up so many advantages, and expose herself to so much ridicule, merely for the sake of protecting abstractions like "culture and intellectual liberty." She answered that this is no matter of abstractions, for brain adultery, the lying and inciting that can be found in every daily newspaper, is another cause of war. If, therefore, outsiders who write were to form themselves into a sect of truthtellers, they would be helping "in the most positive way now open to them . . . to prevent war" (pp. 176-77). These women, the truthtellers, would not, of course, be able to make their opinions heard through the established press, the prostituted press, but it did not follow that they must remain silent. There were other means for propagating one's thoughts "not beyond the reach of a moderate income." There were private printing presses; there were typewriters and duplicators. "By using these cheap and so far unforbidden instruments," they could rid themselves "of the pressure of boards, policies and editors" (p. 177). They could solve the problem of distributing their writings to the public in the manner of other underprivileged societies. "Fling leaflets down basements," Virginia Woolf advised; "expose them on stalls; trundle them along streets on barrows to be sold for a penny or given away. Find out new ways of approaching the 'public' " (p. 178). Further on she suggested that those outsiders who needed to earn their livings might set themselves up as professional truthtellers. They could form a panel of critics to whom writers would go with their literary problems, as they would go to a doctor about their health. Such a service, she reflected, would be well worth a fee of, say, three guineas.

Virginia Woolf was generally adept at mixing different kinds of arguments, but in *Three Guineas* she blurred her theme by persistently emphasizing the profession of literature. She had promised to help her readers confront the realities of world politics, and suddenly she led them into a narrow room. The tone of her admonitions is disturbingly uniform, as if she were failing to acknowledge the fact that there is a difference between a literary skirmish and a real war.

One last article of Virginia Woolf's program—perhaps the most extraordinary of all—was related to professional life. Mothers and wives, she pointed out, perform an essential social function. Domestic life is, in fact, a profession; motherhood is an exacting task and a lofty calling.[16] Outsiders, therefore, "must press for a wage to be paid by the State legally to the mothers of educated men" (p. 200). This would be a fitting recompense for public service, and it would benefit both sexes. It would free married women of their dependence upon their husbands and give them an opportunity to "have a mind and a will of their own" (p. 201). Then it would stimulate the declining birth rate "in the very class where births are desirable—the educated class." Furthermore, Virginia Woolf went on, addressing her argument directly to a hypothetical professional man, "if your wife were paid for her work . . . a real wage, a money wage, so that it became an attractive profession instead of being as it is now an unpaid profession . . . your own slavery would be lightened." She reminded her listener of the crushing burdens he had assumed in order to provide a livelihood for his family; how the pressure of work threatened to turn him into "a cripple in a cave." The salary of the wife could be used to lighten that load. Professional men would no longer find it necessary to go on endlessly augmenting their practices.

---

[16] Virginia Woolf stated this idea earlier in *Night and Day*. "Katharine . . . was a member of a very great profession which has, as yet, no title and very little recognition, although the labor of mill and factory is, perhaps, no more severe and the results of less benefit to the world. She lived at home. She did it very well, too" (p. 44).

"Patients could be sent to the patientless. Briefs to the brief-
less. Articles could be left unwritten. Culture would thus be
stimulated" (p. 202). She concluded by conceding, ironically,
that this plan is, as the politicians say, " 'impracticable' . . .
since three hundred millions or so have to be spent upon the
arm-bearers" (p. 203).

Virginia Woolf's program, as her reference to the arm-
bearers reminds us, originated as an answer to the question:
What can women do to prevent war? She gave relatively
little space, however, to suggestions for direct political action.
The proposals she did make reveal another important assumption, namely, that an antidote to war is to be found in art.
War and art were, in her mind, opposite extremes. War is the
ultimate form of discord; art is the resolution of discord.
War proceeds from intolerance and one-sidedness; art demands the androgynous mind. "If newspapers were written
by people whose sole object in writing was to tell the truth
about politics and the truth about art we should not believe
in war," she maintained, "and we should believe in art"
(p. 176). Accordingly, her political program consists of
radical pacifism and internationalism. Discord is the real
enemy; and the only way to oppose it is to ignore all forms
of violence, keeping one's attention resolutely fixed on some
symbol of harmony, such as a work of art. A course of action
which in any way interfered with the individual's dedication
to his art would have struck her as self-defeating.

Within the limited frame of reference she had chosen,
Virginia Woolf's proposals had their logic. Since love of
one's birthplace, in the form of patriotism, seemed to lead to
the aggravation of national animosities, outsiders should
reject this false claim on their emotions. Their status as
second-class citizens would help them to do this, as it had
helped them in making other renunciations. Virginia Woolf
denied that England, which had deprived women of rights,
was entitled to their help in waging war. The sympathies of
women, she argued, are too broad to be contained within
national boundaries, and "the outsider will say, 'in fact . . . I
have no country. As a woman I want no country. As a
woman my country is the whole world' " (p. 197). If some

scraps of nationalist prejudice remained, outsiders could dispel them by comparing "English painting with French painting; English music with German music; English literature with Greek literature" (pp. 196–97). Considering their cosmopolitan sympathies, outsiders would be unlikely indeed to harbor attitudes that might lead to war. It was scarcely necessary to ask them "not to fight with arms" (p. 193). Virginia Woolf hoped, further, that "they would refuse in the event of war to make munitions or nurse the wounded." But their effectiveness here would be slight, since these duties were, for the most part, "discharged by the daughters of working men." The really arduous task facing outsiders lay, rather, in the psychological realm. They must train themselves "not to incite their brothers to fight, or to dissuade them, but to maintain an attitude of complete indifference" (p. 194). Women cannot understand the instinct to fight, and they should avoid meddling with what they do not understand. They should preserve their detachment. Virginia Woolf saw "indifference" as the only effective way to work for peace, and she saw all interference as a kind of encouragement to the instincts of aggression. In advocating a policy similar to Gandhian noncooperation she was applying the principle, associated with the Mahatma, of not borrowing one's ammunition from the enemy. Furthermore, Virginia Woolf's preaching of "indifference" is reminiscent of popular child psychology and the notion that the best way to discourage a nuisance is to ignore it. "The small boy struts and trumpets outside the window," she wrote; "implore him to stop; he goes on; say nothing; he stops" (p. 199). This policy of "indifference" would entail, once again, many minor renunciations. The outsider would "bind herself to take no share in patriotic demonstrations; to assent to no form of national self-praise . . . to absent herself from military displays, tournaments, tattoos, prize-givings and all such ceremonies as encourage the desire to impose 'our' civilization or 'our' dominion upon other people" (p. 198). The possibility that outsiders might go further, and refuse to bear children, is suggested in a footnote to *Three Guineas.* Virginia Woolf concluded that "the fact that the birth rate in the educated class is falling would seem to show that educated women" have already adopted Lysistrata's policy (p. 266). Finally, it was important that outsiders avoid becoming too conspicuous. "Secrecy is essential," she warned. "We must still hide what we are doing and thinking" (p. 217). For most women were still dependent for their livings upon the establishment, and their interests too must be protected.

Virginia Woolf stipulated that the undertakings of outsiders were to be performed individually, rather than collectively; they should "experiment not with public means in public but with private means in private" (p. 206). The Outsiders' Society was to be a society in name only, "without office, meetings, leaders or any hierarchy, without so much as a form to be filled up, or a secretary to be paid" (p. 209). It was no more, in short, than a convenient catchword referring to the combined effects of many individual acts of protest. Virginia Woolf's program was a blueprint for individual action. In this respect it derived from her attitude as an artist. In the last analysis, both her aesthetic and her feminist principles were governed by a belief in self-reliance, a kind of extreme protestantism. No intermediary, no outer authority, should interpose between the individual and his conscience. Each outsider must stand in a direct relation to the source of the moral imperative, in all the loneliness of her integrity. This emphasis on individual action is closely related to the belief—often reiterated in Virginia Woolf's fiction—that changes in the outer world have little value without a corresponding change of heart. The first responsibility of the individual is to perfect himself. Self-reform is the only kind of reform of whose effect one can be certain, the only kind in which the reformer's motives are above suspicion. Virginia Woolf did not deny all value to the work of the reform societies, but she could not accept the idea that committee work is the best means for furthering the good of mankind, or even for promoting social welfare.

But if the individual outsider was to be guided solely by her own conscience, and charged with the duty of realizing herself, to what extent could she be expected to stay on course toward that goal? Was there some point of reference, a higher court to which she could submit her case when she was in doubt? Virginia Woolf said that there are two "psychometers" upon which the outsider should rely for further guidance. The first is personal, and is equivalent to conscience. The image by means of which Virginia Woolf described this private psychometer casts further light upon her thinking. This psychometer, she wrote, is the one "that you carry on your wrist, the little instrument upon which you depend in all personal relationships. If it were visible it would look something like a thermometer. It has a vein of quicksilver in it which is affected by any body or soul, house or society in whose presence it is exposed" (p. 147). This image of the sensitive vein in the wrist suggests that the outsider should let herself be guided by her first emotional response. In Virginia Woolf's view, being true to one's feelings is a high moral obligation. In addition, however, the outsider should take a reading on the other psychometer, the public psychometer, which would reveal the collective intuition, just as the first had registered her own private intuition. The second psychometer is read by consulting works of art. Great classics are oracles of morality, for art expresses the conscience of mankind. Virginia Woolf proposed the *Antigone* once again, as an example. Sophocles' portrayal of Creon, she said, embodies essential truths about the relations of the citizen and the state. It contains "a far more instructive analysis of tyranny than any our politicians can offer," and can guide the outsider as to "the duties of the individual to society" (p. 148). Obviously, in consulting these two psychometers, the final arbiter is the individual. As a moralist, Virginia Woolf stated no absolutes. Her program was to be carried out in private, and to be based, ultimately, on subjective judgments.

2

In *The Years* Virginia Woolf transformed her ideological uncertainties into art. Rather than attempting to manufacture a program, she dramatized a quest. Throughout the book, her characters ask themselves simple fundamental questions about the individual and society. "If we don't know ourselves, how can we know other people? . . . How can we make laws, religions, that fit?" "[Is] solitude good; [is] society bad?" Although *The Years* differs from *Three Guineas* in formulating questions rather than answers, it deals with the same social crisis, even betrays an interest in ideology. The origin of the book also reveals this interest. In manuscript it originally bore the subtitle: "A novel based upon a paper read to the London National Society for Women's Service."[17] The paper referred to was "Professions for Women," a feminist essay. More than any of Virginia Woolf's other novels, *The Years* grew directly out of her feminism. But though it began as an essay about women in quest of work, it ended as the saga of their lives. Virginia Woolf was not describing contemporary decadence merely in order to prove a point. She was revealing her characters and their world.

Soon after setting to work she "entirely remodelled [her] 'Essay.' It's to be an Essay-Novel, called *The Pargiters*—and it's to take in everything, sex, education, life." As the work progressed she planned to incorporate "millions of ideas but no preaching—history, politics, feminism, art, literature—in short a summing up of all I know." At the same time she was also beginning to express her indignation more directly in *Three Guineas*. But the separation between the work of art and the polemic was never complete. Till the end she felt that *The Years* was "dangerously near propaganda"—so much so that she resolved, as she wrote the final scenes, to avoid glancing at *Three Guineas* lest its influence upset the delicate balance she was trying to achieve in the novel. "One can't propagate at the same time as write fiction," she concluded.[18]

17 See John D. Gordan, "New in the Berg Collection: 1959–1961, Part III," *Bulletin of the New York Public Library* (February, 1964), p. 78.
18 *A Writer's Diary*, November 2, 1932, p. 183; April 25, 1933, p. 191; April 13, 1935, p. 236.

If Virginia Woolf permitted *The Years* to get "dangerously near propaganda," she did so in order to close the gap between stream-of-consciousness and social consciousness. Her ambition, she wrote in her diary, was to have "*The Waves* going on simultaneously with *Night and Day*," that is, to create a new medium in which she could combine poetry and realism. Elsewhere, criticizing D. H. Lawrence for system-mongering, she expressed her goal in terms of a paradox. She imagined discovering a "system that did not shut out."[19] Such a "system" would express both the rational and the intuitive sides of the mind. It would consecrate the union of the young man and young woman riding in her symbolic taxi. That is what she set out to do in *The Years*.

James Hafley has given an excellent summary of her achievement. In comparing the closing scenes of *The Years* and *To the Lighthouse* he points out that "*To the Lighthouse* concludes when Lily Briscoe, exhausted but triumphant, says, 'I have had my vision' and puts aside her paintbrush. *The Years*, on the other hand, concludes with Eleanor reaching out, asking, 'And now?' The present moment is no longer simply an end in itself; it is at once an end and a means."[20] Through her portrayal of Eleanor, in other words, Virginia Woolf has achieved a more satisfactory—because more inclusive—rendering of experience. The visionary heroine is not, as in some poetic novels, cut off from the life of "Monday or Tuesday," but moves in the real world, feeling herself subject to its laws, involved in its problems. "Eleanor as one individual realizes the present moment [Hafley concludes] . . . she has grasped the total meaning of her own life. But Eleanor as a member of society, the public as distinct from the private Eleanor, must perceive her knowledge as means rather than end. . . . The private Eleanor can say that she has had her vision; the public Eleanor, recognizing that vision as a means, must ask, 'And now?'"[21]

Private and public Eleanors can almost be seen as the pro-

19   *Ibid*, April 25, 1933, p. 191; October 2, 1932, pp. 182–83.
20   *The Glass Roof: Virginia Woolf as Novelist* (Berkeley, 1954), p. 144.
21   *Ibid.*, p. 144.

tagonists of two different books. By fusing together symbolic romance and social novel, Virginia Woolf was able to solve an artistic problem that had previously baffled her. In her earlier fiction she had focused mainly on inner experiences because she had not yet found a point of view that enabled her to reconcile public and private worlds. This narrow focus had limited the scope of her canvas. Now, in her portrait of Eleanor, she was able to give both aspects of the personality— solitary and social selves—equal weight. *The Years* demonstrates that every statement about the outer life is also a statement about the inner life. The coins in Eleanor's hand reflect not only a social self seeking to pay her cab fare, but a solitary soul overcoming her egoism. My relation to other people shapes my inner being, and conversely, my inner being determines my capacity for meaningful social relations. Life is a constant process of mediation between contrasting realities.

This twofold awareness pervades *The Years*. It is inherent in the thinking of the main characters, in the imagery used to describe their deepest aspirations. North, for example, dreaming of a "life modelled . . . on the spring of the hard leaping fountain," is aware of a longing "to keep the emblems and tokens of North Pargiter . . . but at the same time spread out, make a new ripple in human consciousness . . . [realize] myself and the world together" (p. 410). Eleanor, reading in bed at night is moved by a different form of this idea in the *Purgatorio*:

> chè per quanti si dice più lì nostro
> tanto possiede più di ben ciascuno. . . .
>
> For by so many more there are who say 'ours'
> So much the more of good doth each possess.

The words, she reflects, do not "give out their full meaning, but [seem] to hold something furled up in the hard shell of the archaic Italian" (pp. 212–13). They are, as it were, another mark on the wall.

Virginia Woolf's "system that did not shut out" represented the same collaboration of masculine intellect and feminine intuition which she had called androgyny in another context. The rational mind, insisting that the individual is merely an insignificant fraction of society, can free us from the tyranny of the ego. Poetic imagination, proclaiming that he is unique—the sum of all things—can free us from the tyranny of social conventions. Eleanor, in her wisdom, has succeeded in combining these different kinds of knowledge. She has integrated her personality. This is the experience that lies behind her serene happiness. And the simple words of the narrative convey it perfectly. "There must be another life. ... Not in dreams; but here and now, in this room, with living people. . . . She hollowed her hands in her lap. . . . She felt that she wanted to enclose the present moment; to make it stay; to fill it fuller and fuller with the past, the present and the future, until it shone, whole, bright, deep with understanding" (pp. 427-28). The image of the mystic sphere shaped by the hollowed hands of the old woman suggests another beacon, a different kind of lighthouse. The very familiarity of the image reminds us that the "other life" must be sought "here and now." Knowledge of a luminous something beyond time, "whole, bright, deep with understanding," can only be attained "in this room, with living people."

The difference between *The Years* and *Three Guineas* is not merely the difference between a work of art and a polemic. It is the difference—to use a psychological metaphor—between a healthy book and a neurotic one. In *The Years* Virginia Woolf avoided self-deceptions and moral ambiguities by expressing her social consciousness in an appropriate form. She fixed her eyes on symbols of inner and outer harmony—glowing coins, a couple riding in a taxi—and with the help of these talismans she was able to face the evil that had traumatized her in *Three Guineas*. She was deeply shocked by the nightmare of history—dead bodies, ruined houses—but she had found a guide through the inferno. Eleanor, whose name means "light," shows the way in which wholeness can be achieved, even in the midst of political and social disintegration.

Virginia Woolf's development as a novelist was deeply influenced by her struggle to reconcile feminism and art.

Long before the aesthetic creed of Bloomsbury came into being she had learned from her father that a work of literature is no better than the morality which it is intended to express— a lesson she never forgot. Virginia Woolf was a passionate moralist, though she directed all her fervor into one narrow channel. The impulse to write *Three Guineas* possessed her for years, "violently . . . persistently, pressingly, compulsorily," until she carried it into action.[22] This moral fervor was not contained within the limits of her tracts, nor could it have been. Feminism is implicit in her novels. The novels are not, of course, didactic in the narrow sense of pleading for specific reforms, but they illustrate the dangers of one-sidedness and celebrate the androgynous mind.

Virginia Woolf's main emphasis in her feminist writings, as in the novels, was on self-reform, and on art as a means to that end. Novels and tracts alike grew out of a preoccupation with her own spiritual dilemma. Fiction was the medium within which Virginia Woolf controlled and directed this intense self-absorption. When she deserted art for propaganda, as in *Three Guineas*, her self-absorption got the upper hand. Thus, paradoxically, she was truer to her feminist ideas as a novelist than as a pamphleteer. Her social conscience and her aesthetic vision were mutually dependent. She could express her feminism only by means of her art; but her art owed its character to her feminism.

The contrast between Virginia Woolf's failure in *Three Guineas* and her triumph in *The Years* confirms this impression. In the first, confining herself to political and social controversy, she lost her grasp of reality and ended by speaking to herself. In the second, striving, as she said, "to give the whole of the present society . . . facts as well as the vision,"[23] she transcended purely personal preoccupations and created a lasting work of art. Virginia Woolf's direct attack on social evil is too shrill and self-indulgent to succeed, even as propaganda. On the other hand, her symbolic representation of the Wasteland—pollution, faithlessness, remorse—has

[22]   *A Writer's Diary*, April 11, 1938, p. 278.
[23]   *Ibid.*, April 25, 1933, p. 191.

a lucid objectivity that forces the reader to see through her eyes. The tract, with all its talk of reform, is one-sided. The novel is whole.

In Virginia Woolf's case, the myth of the artist as more or less helpless agent of his own creative drive seems to have a foundation in fact. She needed the discipline of art, because it permitted her to express her intense moral indignation, while at the same time controlling the disintegrating effects of that indignation upon her personality. Art produced feelings of release and harmony, such as she associated with the androgynous mind. When she avoided that discipline, as in *Three Guineas*, her writing tended to become morbid. In relation to the radiance of Virginia Woolf's artistic successes, therefore, *Three Guineas* represents a kind of negative definition. Through it we can glance into the heart of her darkness.

The feminist rationale of the fiction enabled Virginia Woolf to bind together real and imagined worlds. But the presence of social ideas beneath the surface of a novel can distort, as well as strengthen, the narrative structure. This is particularly true of symbolic fiction. It was Virginia Woolf's most serious weakness as an artist that she occasionally failed to integrate moral and aesthetic designs. Some critics have mistakenly interpreted this failure as an attempt to do away with design altogether, to narrow vision down "to the elementary conditions of momentary experience."[24] Her novels may at first glance give the impression that she was recording incidents and sensations at random, but she never actually did so. The elements of her fiction are always carefully selected and ordered into meaningful patterns. Virginia Woolf was, in the last analysis, a highly intellectual writer. She had observed, however, that over-cultivation of the intellect was extremely common in the world around her,

[24]   D. S. Savage, "The Mind of Virginia Woolf," *South Atlantic Quarterly Review* (October, 1947), p. 560. Cf. W. H. Mellers' attack on Virginia Woolf in his review of *The Years*, "Mrs. Woolf and Life," reprinted in *The Importance of Scrutiny*, ed. Eric Bentley (New York, 1948), pp. 378–82.

and that this kind of gigantism leads to a drying up of the soul. She fought against it.

Virginia Woolf's art celebrates a kind of golden mean, represented by the integrated personality in which thought and feeling are harmoniously combined. Approaching that ideal, her prose becomes luminous. Her novels at their best reveal the intense perceptions of an "exquisite sensibility" in the clear light of universal ideas.

Bibliography

For the works of Virginia Woolf, see *A Bibliography of Virginia Woolf* by B. J. Kirkpatrick (London, 1957).

The following studies contain extensive lists of secondary sources: James Hafley, *The Glass Roof* (Berkeley, 1954); Jean Guiguet, *Virginia Woolf et son Oeuvre* (Paris, 1963). See also "Criticism of Virginia Woolf: A Selected Checklist with an Index to Studies of Separate Works," compiled by Maurice Beebe, *Modern Fiction Studies* (February, 1956), pp. 36–45.

The present study is based upon Virginia Woolf's published work. The Berg Collection of the New York Public Library now includes a large collection of manuscript materials relating to many of her books.

I

By Virginia Woolf

(Where an edition other than the first has been used, the original date of publication is given in parentheses.)

Between the Acts. New York: Harcourt, Brace, 1941.

The Captain's Death Bed and Other Essays. London: Hogarth Press, 1950.

The Common Reader. New York: Harcourt, Brace, 1925.

Bibliography

The Common Reader. 2nd ser. London: Hogarth Press, 1948 (1932).
Contemporary Writers. New York: Harcourt, Brace and World, 1966.
"A Cookery Book," Review of *The Cookery Book of Lady Clark of Tillypronie,* edited by Catherine Frances Frere. *TLS,* November 25, 1909, p. 457.
The Death of the Moth and Other Essays. New York: Harcourt, Brace, 1942.
Flush: A Biography. New York: Harcourt, Brace, 1933.
Granite and Rainbow: Essays. London: Hogarth Press, 1958.
A Haunted House and Other Short Stories. London: Hogarth Press, 1953 (1943).
"The Intellectual Status of Women." Letter to the editor, *New Statesman,* October 16, 1920, pp. 45-46.
"Introduction," *Mrs. Dalloway.* New York: Modern Library, 1928.
Jacob's Room. London: Hogarth Press, 1960 (1922).
"Julia Margaret Cameron." Introduction to *Victorian Photographs of Famous Men and Fair Women,* by Julia Margaret Cameron. London: Hogarth Press, 1926.
"Lady Hester Stanhope." Review of *Lady Hester Stanhope,* by Mrs. Charles Roundell. *TLS,* January 20, 1910, p. 20.
"Men and Women." Review of *La Femme anglaise au XIXe Siècle et son Evolution d'après le Roman anglais contemporain,* by Leonie Villard. *TLS,* March 18, 1920, p. 182.
The Moment and Other Essays. London: Hogarth Press, 1952 (1947).
Monday or Tuesday. New York: Harcourt, Brace, 1921.
"More Carlyle Letters." Review of *The Love Letters of Thomas Carlyle and Jane Welsh,* edited by Alexander Carlyle. *TLS,* April 1, 1909, p. 126.
Mrs. Dalloway. London: Hogarth Press, 1960 (1925).
Night and Day. New York: Harcourt, Brace, 1931 (1919).
Orlando: A Biography. New York: Harcourt, Brace, 1928.
Roger Fry: A Biography. New York: Harcourt, Brace, 1940.
A Room of One's Own. New York: Harcourt, Brace, 1929.
"A Scribbling Dame." Review of *The Life and Romances of Mrs. Eliza Haywood,* by George Frisbie Whicher. *TLS,* February 17, 1916, p. 78.
Three Guineas. London: Hogarth Press, 1952 (1938).
To the Lighthouse. New York: Harbrace Modern Classics, 1959 (1927).
Virginia Woolf and Lytton Strachey: Letters. Edited by Leonard Woolf and James Strachey. New York: Harcourt, Brace, 1956.
The Voyage Out. New York: Blue Ribbon Books, 1920 (1915).

The Waves. London: Hogarth Press, 1955 (1931).
A Writer's Diary (Extracts from the Diary of Virginia Woolf). Edited by Leonard Woolf. New York: Harcourt, Brace, 1953.
The Years. New York: Harcourt, Brace, 1937.

2

Secondary Sources

Aiken, Conrad. "The Novel as Work of Art." Review of *To the Lighthouse. Dial* 83 (July, 1927): 41-44.
Allen, Grant. *The Woman Who Did.* Boston: Roberts Bros., 1895.
Annan, Noël Gilroy. *Leslie Stephen: His Thought and Character in Relation to His Time.* Cambridge, Mass.: Harvard University Press, 1952.
Baldanza, Frank. "Orlando and the Sackvilles." *PMLA* 70 (March, 1955): 274-79.
Beauvoir, Simone de. *The Second Sex.* Translated and edited by H. M. Parshley. New York: Knopf, 1953.
Bell, Clive. *Civilization: An Essay.* New York: Harcourt, Brace, 1928.
———. *Old Friends: Personal Recollections.* New York: Harcourt, Brace, 1957.
———. "Virginia Woolf." *Dial* 67 (December, 1924): 451-65.
Bennett, Joan. *Virginia Woolf: Her Art as a Novelist.* Cambridge: At the University Press, 1945.
Blackstone, Bernard. *Virginia Woolf.* London: British Council, 1952.
———. *Virginia Woolf: A Commentary.* New York: Harcourt, Brace, 1949.
Blease, W. Lyon. *The Emancipation of English Women.* London: David Nutt, 1913.
Brewster, Dorothy. *Virginia Woolf.* New York: Gotham Library, 1962.
———. *Virginia Woolf's London.* New York: New York University Press, 1960.
Brittain, Vera. *Lady into Woman: A History of Women from Victoria to Elizabeth II.* London: Andrew Dakers, 1953.
Browning, Elizabeth Barrett. *Aurora Leigh,* in *Poetical Works,* vol. 5. New York: Dodd, Mead, 1885.
Burgum, Edwin Berry. "Virginia Woolf and the Empty Room," *The Novel and the World's Dilemma.* New York: Oxford University Press, 1947.
Cecil, David. *Dictionary of National Biography,* s.v. "Woolf, Virginia."

Chambers, R. L. *The Novels of Virginia Woolf*. Edinburgh: Oliver and Boyd, 1947.

Daiches, David. "Virginia Woolf," *The Novel and the Modern World*. Rev. ed. Chicago: University of Chicago Press, 1960.

———. *Virginia Woolf*. Norfolk, Conn.: New Directions, 1942.

Delattre, Floris. *Le Roman psychologique de Virginia Woolf*. Paris: Libraire Philosophique J. Vrin, 1932.

Eliot, T. S. "Virginia Woolf." *Horizon* 3 (May, 1941): 313–16.

Fawcett, Millicent Garrett. *Women's Suffrage: A Short History of a Great Movement*. London: T. C. and E. C. Jack, n. d.

Forster, E. M. "The Early Novels of Virginia Woolf," *Abinger Harvest*. New York: Harcourt, Brace, 1936.

———. *Howards End*. Harmondsworth: Penguin Books, 1941.

———. *A Passage to India*. New York: Harcourt, Brace, 1924.

———. *Virginia Woolf: The Rede Lecture*. Cambridge: At the University Press, 1942. Reprinted in *Two Cheers for Democracy*. New York: Harcourt, Brace, 1951.

Freedman, Ralph. "Awareness and Fact: The Lyrical Vision of Virginia Woolf," *The Lyrical Novel*. Princeton: Princeton University Press, 1963.

Grant, Duncan. "Virginia Woolf." *Horizon* (June, 1941), pp. 402–6.

Greene, Graham. "From the Mantelpiece." Review of *Three Guineas*. *Spectator*, June 17, 1938, pp. 1110–12.

Gruber, Ruth. *Virginia Woolf: A Study*. Leipzig: Bernhard Tauchnitz, 1935.

Guiget, Jean. *Virginia Woolf et son oeuvre*. Paris: Didier, 1963. Translated by Jean Stewart as *Virginia Woolf and Her Works*. New York: Harcourt, Brace and World, 1966.

Hafley, James. *The Glass Roof: Virginia Woolf as Novelist*. Berkeley and Los Angeles: University of California Press, 1954.

Harding, Esther. *Woman's Mysteries*. New York: Pantheon, 1955.

Harrod, R. F. "Bloomsbury." In *John Maynard Keynes*. New York: Harcourt, Brace, 1951.

Hollingworth, Keith. "Freud and the Riddle of *Mrs. Dalloway*." In *Studies in Honor of John Wilcox*. Detroit: Wayne State University Press, 1958.

Holtby, Winifred. *Virginia Woolf*. London: Wishart, 1932.

Humphrey, Robert. *Stream of Consciousness in the Modern Novel*. Berkeley and Los Angeles: University of California Press, 1959.

Hungerford, Edward A. "Mrs. Woolf, Freud and J. D. Beresford." *Literature and Psychology* 5 (August, 1955): 49–51.

Hunting, Constance. "Technique in *Orlando*." *Modern Fiction Studies* 2 (February, 1956): 17–22.

John, K. "The New Lysistrata." Review of *Three Guineas. New Statesman and Nation*, June 11, 1938, pp. 995-96.

Johnstone, J. K. *The Bloomsbury Group*. London: Secker and Warburg, 1954.

Kallich, Martin. *The Psychological Milieu of Lytton Strachey*. New York: New York Bookman Associates, 1961.

Kelsey, Mary Electa. "Virginia Woolf and the She-Condition." *Sewanee Review* (October–December, 1931), pp. 425-44.

Keynes, John Maynard. "My Early Beliefs," *Essays and Sketches in Biography*. New York: Meridian Books, 1956.

Kirkpatrick, B. J. *A Bibliography of Virginia Woolf*. London: Rupert Hart-Davis, 1957.

Leavis, Q. D. "Caterpillars of the Commonwealth, Unite." Review of *Three Guineas. Scrutiny* 7 (September, 1938). Reprinted in *The Importance of Scrutiny*, edited by Eric Bentley. New York: G. W. Stewart, 1948.

Lehmann, John. *I Am My Brother*. New York: Harcourt, Brace, 1960.

――――. *The Whispering Gallery*. New York: Harcourt, Brace, 1954.

Macaulay, Rose. "Virginia Woolf." *Horizon* 3 (May, 1941): 316-18.

MacCarthy, Desmond. *Memories*. London: Oxford University Press, 1953.

Maitland, F. W. *The Life and Letters of Leslie Stephen*. London: Duckworth, 1906.

Marder, Herbert. "Beyond the Lighthouse: *The Years*," *Bucknell Review* 15, no. 1 (March, 1967): 61-70.

Meller, W. H. "Mrs. Woolf and Life." Review of *The Years*. Reprinted in *The Importance of Scrutiny*, edited by Eric Bentley. New York: G. W. Stewart, 1948.

Mill, John Stuart. *The Subjection of Women*. London: Everyman, 1929.

Mitford, Nancy, ed. *Noblesse Oblige: An Enquiry into the Identifiable Characteristics of the English Aristocracy*. London: H. Hamilton, 1956.

Mortimer, Raymond. "Virginia Woolf," *Channel Packet*. London: Hogarth Press, 1942.

Nathan, Monique. *Virginia Woolf*. Translated by Herma Briffault. New York: Evergreen Books, 1961.

"Night and Day." Reviewed in *TLS*, October 31, 1919, p. 607.

Norton, Caroline. *English Laws for Women in the Nineteenth Century*. London, 1854. (Printed for private circulation.)

Overcarsh, F. L. "The Lighthouse, Face to Face." *Accent* (Winter, 1950), pp. 107-23.

Bibliography

Page, Alex. "Mrs. Dalloway Discovers Her Double." *Modern Fiction Studies* 7 (Summer, 1961): 115-24.

Pippett, Aileen. *The Moth and the Star: A Biography of Virginia Woolf.* Boston: Little, Brown, 1955.

Plomer, William. "Virginia Woolf." *Horizon* 3 (May, 1941): 323-27.

Ridley, Hilda. "Leslie Stephen's Daughter." *Dalhousie Review* 33 (Spring, 1953): 65-72.

Roberts, J. H. "Toward Virginia Woolf." *Virginia Quarterly Review* (October, 1934), pp. 587-602.

———. "'Vision and Design' in Virginia Woolf." *PMLA* 61 (1946): 835-47.

Sackville-West, Victoria. *Knole and the Sackvilles.* London: W. Heinemann, 1922.

———. "Virginia Woolf." *Horizon* 3 (May, 1941): 318-23.

———. "Virginia Woolf and Orlando." *Listener,* January 27, 1955, pp. 157-58.

Savage, D. S. "The Mind of Virginia Woolf." *South Atlantic Quarterly Review* (October, 1947), pp. 556-73.

Schaefer, Josephine O' Brien. *The Three-fold Nature of Reality in the Novels of Virginia Woolf.* The Hague: Mouton, 1965.

Seward, Barbara. *The Symbolic Rose.* New York: Columbia University Press, 1960.

Simon, Irene. "Some Aspects of Virginia Woolf's Imagery." *English Studies* 41, no. 3 (June, 1960): 180-96.

Spender, Stephen. "The Life of Literature." *Partisan Review* (January, 1949), pp. 188-92.

Steinberg, Erwin R. "Freudian Symbolism and Communication." *Literature and Psychology* 3 (April, 1953): 2-5.

Stephen, Leslie. *Hours in a Library.* 4 vols. New York and London: Knickerbocker Press, 1904.

———. *Social Rights and Duties.* 2 vols. London: Swan, Sonnenschein, 1896.

Strachey, Ray. *The Cause: A Short History of the Women's Movement in Great Britain.* London: G. Bell and Sons, 1928.

———. (ed.) *Our Freedom and Its Results.* London: Hogarth Press, 1936.

Sudrann, Jean. "The Sea, the City and the Clock: A Study of Symbolic Form in the Novels of Virginia Woolf." Ph.D. dissertation, Columbia, 1950.

Tindall, William York. *Forces in Modern British Literature.* New York: Vintage Books, 1956.

———. *The Literary Symbol.* New York: Columbia University Press, 1955.

————. "Many-Levelled Fiction: Virginia Woolf to Ross Lockridge." *College English* 10 (November, 1948): 65-71.

Toynbee, Philip. "Virginia Woolf: A Study of Three Experimental Novels." *Horizon* (November, 1946), pp. 290-304.

Troy, William. "Virginia Woolf, I: The Poetic Method." *Symposium* (January, 1932).

————. "Virginia Woolf, II: The Poetic Style." *Symposium* (April, 1932).

Walpole, Hugh. "Virginia Woolf." *New Statesman and Nation*, June 14, 1941, p. 603.

Wells, H. G. *Ann Veronica*. New York: Harper, 1909.

Wollstonecraft, Mary. *A Vindication of the Rights of Women*. London: Everyman, 1929.

The Woman Question. Edited by T. R. Smith. New York: Modern Library, 1918.

Woolf, Leonard. *Sowing: An Autobiography of the Years 1880-1904*. New York: Harcourt, Brace, 1960.

————. *Growing: An Autobiography of the Years 1904-1911*. New York: Harcourt, Brace, 1962.

————. *Beginning Again: An Autobiography of the Years 1911 to 1918*. New York: Harcourt, Brace, 1964.

Wyatt, Frederick. "Some Comments on the Use of Symbols in the Novel." *Literature and Psychology* (April, 1953), pp. 15-23.

Index

Index

Eliot, George, 34, 70, 122
Eliot, T. S., 120–21

Fascism, 28, 97
Feminist societies: WSPU (the
    militants), 18–19; V. Woolf's
    attitude to, 20, 22, 29–30, 91–94,
    98, 106; hostility to, 29; and
    anti-fascists, 96–97; in *The
    Years*, 100–101
Flush, 81–82
Forster, E. M., 97, 119 n.; on
    V. Woolf's feminism, 1, 30; on
    V. Woolf's attitude to class, 84
Freedman, Ralph, 126

Galsworthy, 117–20 *passim*
Gandhi, 168
Georgian novel, 119–21
Gosse, Edmond, 59

Hafley, James, 52, 126; on Mrs.
    Ramsay, 40; on *Night and Day*,
    56, 92; on *Orlando*, 116; on the
    lighthouse, 146; on *The Years*,
    172.
Hardy, Thomas, 8
Holtby, Winifred, 116 n., 126,
    139 n.
Hunting, Constance, 115 n.

Ibsen, 7–8

Jacob's Room, 81, 83; symbolism
    in, 98–99, 137–38
Joyce, James, 64, 120, 121

Keynes, John Maynard, 17
Kipling, 117

"Laetitia Pilkington," 137 n.
Lawrence, D. H., 2, 172
"Leaning Tower, The," 84 n.
Leavis, Q. D., 156
Lighthouse; *see* Symbolism
Literary criticism (by V. Woolf):
    and feminism, 25–26; and
    androgyny, 117–25; and new
    feminine fiction, 122–25

"Mark on the Wall, The," 87–88,
    108, 146; and androgyny,
    130–33
Marriage; *see* Domestic life;
    Symbolism
Married Women's Property Act,
    The, 6

"Memories of a Working
    Women's Guild," 87 n.
"Modern Fiction," 120, 142 n.
"Mr. Bennett and Mrs. Brown,"
    31–32, 117, 118–19
Mrs. Dalloway, 23–24, 39–40,
    41 n., 86 n., 88 n., 99, 134; the
    patriarchy in, 48–50, 94–96

Night and Day, 21–22, 23, 32–33,
    34–35, 38–39, 41, 46, 88, 108,
    117 n., 127, 129, 135, 138 n.,
    150 n., 166 n., 172; symbolism
    in, 36, 139–42, 142–44; solitude
    and society in, 53–54, 56;
    biographical significance, 55 n.;
    suffrage society in, 92–94;
    androgyny in, 128
Nightingale, Florence, 34

Orlando, 15, 24, 26, 27, 70–71,
    71–72, 76, 142 n.; androgyny
    in, 110–16; symbolism in,
    135–36
Overcarsh, F. L., 40

Pankhurst, Emmeline, 18–19
Patriarchy: and the Victorians,
    3, 46–47, 131–32; and Leslie
    Stephen, 9–16 *passim*; evils of,
    23–24, 83–91; and the
    professions, 33–34, 78, 90,
    163–67; in V. Woolf's novels,
    46–53 *passim*; and ceremonial
    dress, 85–86; satirized in
    Orlando, 111–13
Pippett, Aileen, 56 n., 107 n.,
    112 n., 126
Plomer, William, 126 n.

188

Index

Wells, H. G., 8, 118-20 *passim*
Wollstonecraft, Mary, 54-55,
   83 n.
Women: status of, 5-7, 66-67;
   and the social code, 41-43; as
   outsiders, 67, 86, 97-98, 157-58,
   159-70; grievances summarized,
   69-82; writers, 69-71, 117,
   121-25, 164-66; education of,
   72-75, 159-61; poverty of,
   75-78; and childbearing, 77-78;
   and the professions, 78, 163-67;
   lack of influence of, 78; as an
   oppressed class, 79-82; and
   minorities, 80-82; economic
   emancipation of, 98; discover
   their identity, 106-7; and
   chastity, 114; moral superiority

of, 158-59; and patriotism, 67,
   167-69
"Women and Fiction," 32 n., 34,
   71
"Women Novelists," 121 n.
Woolf, Leonard, 19-20, 56 n.
Writer's Diary, A, 103 n., 107 n.;
   on *The Years*, 171-72

Years, The, 4, 26, 64, 130, 146,
   156-57, 162, 175-76;
   summarized, 27-28; symbolism
   in, 36-37, 100-103, 141-42, 145;
   marriage in, 58-63; androgyny
   in, 128-29; compared with *To
   the Lighthouse*, 154-55; as
   ideological novel, 170-74
Yeats, W. B., 2